2020

-

STARTING A BUSINESS

2.0

Henry Cheng

Copyright © Henry Cheng, 2018

The author reserves all the right to this book. They do not permit anyone to reproduce or transmit any part of this book through any means or form be it electronic or mechanical. No one has the right to store the information herein in a retrieval system, or to photocopy, record copies, scan parts, etc., without the proper permission of the publisher or author.

Disclaimer

All the information in this document is to be used for informational and educational purposes only. The author will not account in any way for any results that stem from the use of the information herein. While conscious and creative attempts have been made to ensure that all information provided herein is as accurate and useful as possible, the author is not legally bound to be responsible for any damage caused by the accuracy as well as use/misuse of this information.

DEDICATION

To my loving parents who sacrificed every day, showing us what true work ethic looked like.

Contents

INTRODUCTION

Entrepreneurship is unarguably quite a daunting task, especially for inexperienced newcomers. As such, many individuals with regular jobs that pay them enough to live comfortably are quite reluctant to descend into such a risk-laden territory they are yet to explore or discover. For those who take the plunge, most do so due to unforeseen circumstances. This ingress to unfamiliar territory usually refers to a change in the stability of a "regular job" may be an employer's pay cut or a greater family responsibility such as a new born, etc., a higher standard of living, or even outright loss of job among other possible factors. The more capable and astute individual figure out how to make that leap early on.

Most individuals find themselves starting a business either voluntarily at their own pace or forced into it by situations beyond their control i.e. the need to survive. Of these two scenarios, it is obvious that one outcome is more ideal than the other. The individual in the first scenario is in a better position to prepare himself properly for whatever business he wishes to engage in, however the individual in the second scenario may find the grit, prospective and experience he may need to sustain himself in starting a new business.

In starting a business, preparation is key. Whatever the business it may be, there are important preliminary research that have to be carried out before initiating such a business. This includes, but does not limit to the amount of capital required for the business, what level of expertise (if any) is required, what laid down procedures (if any) exist to guide and regulate the business, what is the profit margin, how long does it take to get desired returns from the business, etc. Failure to perform due diligence before starting a business oftentimes leads to future setbacks and wasted capital, in some cases, it may lead to the premature emotional or financial demise of your business.

One burning question in the minds of most individuals, especially those who have little experience in operating their own business is: *"Why should I choose to undertake the risks and challenges of having a business when I can make a living without it?"*

Well, there are a couple of answers to this question and some of them are:

- **You Can Never Be Richer Than Your Boss**

An everyday worker who depends solely on his salary paying job as his only source of income cannot be richer than his/her boss. It's quite simple really, your boss decides what you get paid, and in most cases, I can assure you he is NEVER going to pay you more than he'll pay himself. Furthermore, if a successful company is hit by hard times, you can be certain that you'll be negatively influenced by the harsh reality than your boss. If you however own some other sources of income in conjunction with your salary paying job, these other sources will serve as a cushion in the day of trouble as well as a boost so maybe, just maybe, you can be on par with your boss.

Being your own boss on the other hand, is the surest route to financial independence. After careful consideration of overhead expenditures, you get to decide where you need to reinvest your revenue in order to support company growth. When you start to see a positive financial gap in the margins between overhead expenditures and revenue you can start to set aside your personal income distribution (If you are the sole owner).

- **The Richest People in The World Work for No One**

Looking through the list of wealthy individuals inscribed in various record books, you will instantly discover one thing - they all have one value creating organisation or the other. These are individuals who have grown their businesses to the point that they have etched their names in the hearts of people around the world and in books of history as well. It should not shock you to know that these wealthy people are oftentimes only responsible for the decision-making process in their respective businesses. The heavy lifting as well as the day to day activities of their businesses are left to be executed by an employee. This leads us to the next point.

- **You Do the Work; Your Boss Takes the Credit**

This is the prevalent albeit sad reality facing the average prospective of an employee. Some even have it stated in their contracts of employment that whatever their employees discover, develop or invent while under the employment of the company is the property of the company. This is one of the forerunning factors that explains why you rarely see famous workers. What you see instead are famous bosses taking the podium to announce a ground-breaking discovery made by an unnamed worker in the name of the company.

If you are seeking something more fulfilling than a salary, bonus, vacation and a pension, then being an employee is something that will not fill your void.

• **Your Kids Cannot Inherit Your Job**

Regardless of how lucrative, pleasant and secure your job is, it only ends with you. At the height of optimism, you put enough aside in a pension, annuity or retirement savings; all to have a fixed monthly retirement income, thinking that will guarantee you a good life. For instance, the first insurance agency that I acquired had a majority of clients in their eighties and nineties who were living on fixed income from retirement plans that they have started funding since they were in their thirties. It was hard to see elderly clients having to struggle day to day while keeping up with the inflating economy at a fixed income.

In many cases, having your own business has its advantages in that it keeps up with inflation and can be sold at market value. It is also a worthy legacy that gives your children options – they can either allow the business to provide generational income or use to build assets that can compound over time.

• Your 9 – 5 Will Most Likely Become 24/7

What is the difference between a Job and Career? For me, a job is something you do temporarily for money, and a career is more like a permanent job... in that you see yourself doing it for the long term.

Average Hours Worked by Full-Time U.S. Workers, Aged 18+

In a typical week, how many hours do you work?

	Employed full-time
	%
60+ hours	18
50 to 59 hours	21
41 to 49 hours	11
40 hours	42
Less than 40 hours	8

Based on Gallup data from the 2013 and 2014 Work and Education polls, conducted in August of each year

GALLUP

Courtesy of gallup.com

The table above shows that 50% of workers in the U.S work more than the 40-hour cap stipulated by federal law. These imposed responsibilities usually create, in most cases, a certain amount of uncertainty for the worker as to his schedule while also taking a negative toll on physical and mental health.

A couple of compelling arguments have been outlined above as to why you should start your own business. For one, you spend majority of your life building another person's dream. If you spend 40 hours a week for ten years, that's 20, 800 hours of time spent dedicated to someone else's vision.

In many cases, being an entrepreneur is more exhausting than working for somebody. The question you have to ask yourself is... "is the fruit worth the squeeze?" In that same ten years, would you be willing to dedicate twice the number of hours to own your dream?

It's easy to see the success in an entrepreneur that built his business from the ground up, but it is hard to see the sacrifices that were made in order to get there. In an emergency, the employee can choose to not pick up the phone after hours... but as the boss you cannot make such a whimsical decision. Operating a business in that manner is irresponsible and a sure way to expedite the failure of a business.

CHAPTER ONE

OVERCOMING THE 9 – 5 RAT RACE

Here are some straight-to-the-point ideas on how you can start to prepare yourself for the big life of being your own boss.

- **Stop Thinking Like an Employee and Start Thinking Like a Boss**

If you study most people with regular 9 – 5 jobs, especially those who have had a steady job for a long time, there's usually this clingy, almost hypnotic fog around them that has them feeling everything is alright as long as they get a steady pay check and regular promotion. This is usually backed up by the instinctual ability of human beings to adapt to most situations. Thus, individuals who work for other people have it ingrained subliminally into them that they are doing just fine as long as they can meet their essential needs conveniently and are not too indebted.

It should therefore not come as much of a surprise that the first element required to escape your 9 – 5 is **Mental Readiness**. Many people have been 'trying' and 'struggling' for years to give their 9 – 5 the slip to no avail. They always bring up an excuse every time to justify the continued stay in their comfortable routine. Excuses like: 'The company's bonuses and benefits are great', 'I need to save more money first', 'I'll do it after the kids graduate', etc. The truth is that there will never be a perfect time for you to take the decision to leave your 9-5 and become your own boss. Just take the bull by the horn and do it afraid. As you continue to procrastinate, your dream of being your own boss dies slowly.

The first test of being a boss is the ability to make tough decisions. A boss, when faced with a tough decision evaluates the risks and the rewards obtainable from the decision, then goes ahead with it if he is comfortable with it. An employee on the other hand, even with the knowledge of the risks and rewards, still requires validation from a higher authority before taking decisions. To disrupt your 9 – 5 rat race mentality, you have to first attune your mind-set to making tough decisions.

- **Find A Societal Want and/or Need for Which You'll Create Value**

While reminiscing about his experience in business, the CEO of Porch, Matt Ehrlichman said; *"In building my company, we realized that the best opportunities are when you can truly help solve another's problem"*. So basically, a business is simply an apparatus created to solve problems and meet the needs of people. For instance, a transport business solves the problem of movement for individuals.

In economics, the concepts of 'Wants' and 'Needs' are similar, they differ however in that while wants cater for our non-essential cravings, needs are required for our very existence as human beings.

In relation to leaving your 9 – 5, you should have a plan for a replacement (usually a business), so you won't find the ground giving way under you at your first step to freedom. To start with, you must first identify wants and or needs in the environment where you seek to set up a business. However, note that it is easier to get patronage for needs (human needs basically include everything relating to food, clothing and shelter) than for wants. On the other hand, humans are more likely to spend more on wants after satisfying their needs.

In identifying the wants or needs you want to cater to, ensure you consider all parameters including how much effort will be required to set up a business around it; how much capital is required to set up the business; how easy or otherwise it'll be to generate patronage; etc. The answers to fundamental questions like these will determine how you will proceed.

For instance, there are businesses that you can run while still working 9 – 5 (at least in the beginning, pending when you are fully prepared to finally quit your job), while there are others that require full-time commitment (these however have to be planned ahead before you quit). Whichever option you choose, you must make smart preparations, which leads us to our next point.

- **Do Your Homework**

Whatever endeavour you choose to venture into, it is highly important that you carry out adequate research before you quit your 9 – 5, so that you won't get stuck in the middle of a venture for lack of adequate planning.

To kick-start your research and planning, you can look to the internet, read books, attend seminars, workshops and conferences for profound insights. You can as well seek advice from entrepreneurs and business owners around you. Never charge headlong into a business without adequate information and preparation. A business has many moving parts that are required for achieving success. Proper analysis in researching competition, supply and demand, workforce and legalities to name a few, are the building blocks of future success.

The importance of this step is such that the success or failure of your business is hinged on it. Many individuals have found themselves struggling with a business they had no concern going into in the first place.

To avoid the heartbreak that failure heralds, ensure you have passion in all of its trials and tribulations. Don't do it just for the money, but essentially because it is what you love to do and are content doing it for the rest of your life. Be sure you get adequate research and plan ahead before you ditch your 9 – 5.

- **Build A Network**

Having the right network of people around you is sure to make your entrepreneurial journey less stressful. As a matter of fact, networking has been identified as the most important unwritten rule of business success. Networking, according to Diane Helbig is *"a big investment in your business. It takes time and when done correctly can yield great results for years to come."* It goes without saying that who you know and who knows you could make your complete transition to the world of entrepreneurship hitch free.

The great thing is, you can build your network even while you're still working your 9 – 5. Forging strategic relationships in the industry you are attempting to penetrate will task your social skills for building strong relationships with your customers, associates and employees and give you an excellent head-start as you take your business off the ground.

- **Leverage on The Resources Available to You**

I daresay, this is a wonderful time to be alive. The magic of technology, internet network and globalization has made the process of starting and running a business quite easy. The difficulty attached with entrepreneurship in the past was one of the factors that limited the number of people entering into business, while it also greatly reduced the success to failure rate of businesses established within that period. Today however, the situation has seen a complete turnaround.; thanks to the advancement of science and technology in leaps and bounds. For instance, you can start a small import business nowadays, with the power of your smart phone. It can be as simple as determining a demand, logging on to alibaba.com to source a supply, and placing an order to meet that demand. If it were to be in times past, our parents and grandparents would have had to take a bus, plane, or boat to a different country and physically be somewhere to negotiate an imported product. The process of idea to inception in those days would have added months to the research and development stage.

The comparative ease of doing business these days doesn't simply end here. You can also get legal counsel, and even professionally drafted contracts from various online services at prices that are relatively cheaper than meeting a lawyer physically.

Furthermore, in the United States of America, and many other progressive countries, registering your business is as simple as visiting the website of the commission in charge of corporate affairs to submit the relevant documents and even make the required payments online.

Furthermore, creating a network of value adding individuals is a piece of cake with modern technology. You can meet and learn from people who have had success in business at various levels via social media.

What I am driving at here is that, owning and running a business nowadays when compared to the days of our parents, is a breeze; thanks to the behemoth of resources and information literally at your fingertips. Make the move and turn a deaf ear to the naysayers who tell you the task is risky. Now is the best and most self-informative time to make educated decisions with little investment. Just with your mobile phone, internet connection and a mind-set filled with motivation, the sky is your limit.

• Know How to Quit

While it is understandable that your move to liberate yourself from your 9 – 5 could be fraught with strong emotions, it is however imperative that your disengagement is as amicable as it can be. Don't burn your bridges. Who says your previous colleagues and bosses cannot be your customers or even part of the network of individuals that can support you and your business.

A common mistake many people transitioning from a 9 – 5 to their own business make is that they treat the job, and the people they met there, like a closed chapter in their lives - never to be revisited. This approach is unadvisable as it could affect you negatively.

Your current boss could give you some important insights about running a business and how to avoid certain pitfalls, which you may not be able to get elsewhere. Therefore, if you decide it's finally time to quit that 9 - 5, do so without straining your relationship with those you met on the job as much as possible.

LESSONS TO LEARN FROM YOUR 9 – 5 JOB

Much as it might be unsustainable to depend on your 9 - 5 job in the long run, your business will suffer and falter if you fail to learn some vital lessons while helping your boss run their business. In other words, unless you are able to leverage your 9 - 5 as a training ground for your entrepreneurship bid, you would definitely be experimenting with some fundamental aspects of your business (at least at inception). This could have devastating effects on your business and if a grave enough mistake is made, it could as well lead to the untimely demise of the business.

So as to forestall the above unfortunate scenario, here are some takeaways from your 9 - 5 that you'll probably need when starting your business:

• **WORK ETHIC:** to have a strong work ethic is to continuously be in a state of mind that extols the benefit and true value of work. An individual with good work ethic knows the importance of hard work and finds joy in pouring his energy into productive work. Such an individual makes it a point to ensure there is no discrepancy in the quality of his work.

Good work ethic is not debatable for the success of any enterprise. In the context of starting your own business, your work ethic is constant both on your 9 – 5 job, and in your personal business. Therefore, if you have a poor work ethic at your 9 – 5, it's either you improve yourself or you'll carry it over to your own business. In fact, in many cases, starting your own business requires even more dedication and laser like focus, painstaking consistency and strong work ethic.

Furthermore, you can hone your soft skills at your 9 – 5. Your 9-5 can be an avenue to improve your leadership, emotional intelligence, and communications skills. While speaking at the 2018 World Economic Forum in Davos, Jack Ma argued that soft and not hard skills are what will stand people out in a world where almost any question can be answered by google. These social skills are the blocks that shape your character, which to a large extent is a core determining factor of business success. Strong human relations skill is something you must have figured out before you launch your business.

• **YOUR JOB DEFINES YOU**: After thorough immersion in a profession, especially the first five years, it should come as no surprise that fundamental components of your being will definitely be influenced by your job. For instance, someone who works as a customer service agent is more likely to be better at dealing with irate individuals than an engineer. A doctor is more likely to be better at showing empathy than a mechanic, etc.

If you think about it very well, it makes sense. You spend about 8 hours at your 9 - 5 job every day, five days a week. That is 40 hours (more or less) of performing similar, repetitive tasks every week. Definitely there will be a transference of traits commonly associated with the job, to the worker. This should assist you in determining the type of business you will excel at and should therefore decide to pursue.

- **THE CUSTOMER IS ALWAYS RIGHT:** The Japanese word for customer, "kyakusama", in English translates to "honoured guest". So, if in the regular process of your job, you get to directly interact with customers, then you'll know that one of the key tenets, or perhaps the only tenet of business success is "the customer is always right". Your boss probably keeps re-emphasising this point to you on a regular basis, and contravening this principle is an unforgiveable sin to him/her.

For those who are not privileged to have direct contact with customers on their jobs, the principle of customer satisfaction means that on no occasion should you argue with a customer or make him feel in the wrong. Always ensure that the customer feels desired, appreciated and honoured, so as to enjoy continued patronage from customers. Businesses that joy in treating customers without respect will certainly lose customers to competitors that treat them well.

This principle is best learnt while you still have someone (a boss, a supervisor, a co-worker, etc.) drumming its importance in your ears. This is because there is a tendency for individuals who do not know how to treat customers right, to not be correctable when they start their own businesses because they are at that point above everyone else in the organisation. The few exceptions are in those who do not mind learning from subordinates.

Good customer service is the bedrock of any business. It determines the kind of patronage you have and how much of it you'd have. A good rule of thumb is to treat every customer as though your business exists at their pleasure, because it actually does.

I am sure that at this point, you now have a grasp of why your 9 - 5 is not a sustainable option. Now that we have examined why you need to own your own business; the ease of starting & running a business in this age, thanks to modern technology; how to amicably disengage from your 9-5 when you are ready to launch and some takeaways from your regular job that will help you in your business, what next?

CHAPTER TWO

THE INTERNET GIVES SLACKERS A CHANCE

It is an undeniable fact that the internet has slowly, gradually but surely taken a major role in various aspects of our lives. We rely on the internet, more than we can realize, for the many things in our lives such as staying up to date on the ever-changing landscape of current events, personal organization, appointment setting, developing self-taught skills and of course, networking - to name some basic few.

The internet has proven its importance in its long list of uses and applications. Apart from its most common use which is for dissemination of information, it can also serve as a means of connecting individuals who otherwise may not have been able to meet in person, thus saving on time and energy. It also enables one to bridge many long-distance relationships. The internet may also be used to enhance both business-related and other non-business-related operations via the numerous tools available online, each serving its specific purpose.

Before the advent and widespread application of the internet, starting and running a business was considerably more daunting. Fundamental aspects of business such as communication, advertising and marketing as well as research required serious commitment, time and effort. With the introduction of the internet into business however, and the development of e-business and e-commerce platforms, even slackers who lack preference for engaging in energy consuming activities can now start and oversee relatively successful businesses with ease.

ASPECTS OF BUSINESS INFLUENCED BY THE INTERNET

- **COMMUNICATION:** This is unarguably one of the areas of business and general life that has been impacted by the internet the most, in comparison to others. Before the advent of the internet, communication as far as business is concerned could only be done either in person, over the phone, or by sending a letter or telegram by post. This made it somewhat difficult for business owner to stay in touch with customers, employees and associates. Moreover, business partners could not quickly contact each other to make necessary decisions as regards the business in times of emergency. As such, the growth and development of businesses in this era was greatly limited, with some suffering a couple of setbacks.

With the advent and widespread usage of the internet however, sending a message via electronic mail does not require either the sender or the receiver to step into a post office. With little time and finance spent, emails are sent and received in seconds via a wide selection of email services. Thus, a business can have its customers on a mailing list and inform them of new products and services in the twinkle of an eye with just the tap of a couple of buttons.

Furthermore, businesses are able to connect with their employees and partners via SMM (social media marketing) by making use of any of the popular social media platforms Facebook, Instagram, and Twitter. Meetings to make important business decisions need not wait till every concerned stakeholder is present physically. With the use of video and conference calls, concerned individuals can partake in the meeting from their preferred locations, with the power of their smartphones at their fingertips while still wearing their pyjamas.

In the book **The World is Flat**, Thomas Friedman while recounting his experience in Bangalore India, stated unequivocally that; *"No matter what your profession – doctor, lawyer, architect, accountant – if you are an American, you better be good at the touchy-*

feely service stuff, because anything that can be digitized can be outsourced to either the smartest or the cheapest producer." One can find professional services online at prices a fraction of what one will pay for a physical service. Business can save a lot of time, effort and resources simply by digitizing their operations.

Another angle to the improvement of communication in business is language. Thanks to globalization, businesses now cut across borders and sometimes a business owner may be required to converse with an individual who speaks a different language from his to make an order, discuss the terms of a deal, gain technical knowledge, etc. Some mobile phone apps such as WeChat and Facebook enables you to translate from one language to another within the messenger.

Thirty years ago, business persons faced with this kind of predicament had to find an interpreter. These mobile apps thus, eliminate the need to go and learn a second language or hire an interpreter before you can transact business.

- **CUSTOMER SERVICE:** Prior to the advent of internet, the traditional methods of resolving customer complaints were simply not as effective. They were long, tedious and placed a considerable economic strain on both the business and customers. Decades ago customers called in or were required to physically visit customer service representatives to lodge complaints. It was also much more expensive as businesses had to create and sustain office space housing more employees, thereby adding to business overhead. With automation, artificial intelligence, and machine learning... customer service can be accessed outside of normal business hours, costs businesses less in wages and has increased customer satisfaction.

In this era of stiff competition, small businesses are competing with the technology budget of large companies by automating services and providing instant gratification to customers. For consumers however, this has definitely improved customer experience.

The internet has changed the narrative and now, even the smallest businesses can operate virtual 24/7 customer service centres. Apart from the obvious cost advantage virtual customer service centres also require very few members of staff as it can be overseen by as little as two people.

Taking it a step further, there are self-care systems called Chatbots that enable customers to resolve complaints without having to rely on human assistance. Thus, customers can resolve simple complaints themselves using user friendly systems.

In the evolution of business software technologies, enhancing customer services has become simpler. It has provided customers of small businesses a level playing field of care and comfort in resolving issues, as they would have enjoyed if they patronise a larger firm.

•   **RESEARCH:** As stated in the first chapter of this book, before you start a business, you have to carry out adequate research to decrease the chances of your business failing within the first year. Some of the past methods of research for a starting a new business involved searching at your local library for the right books and documents, conducting surveys by calling or physically approaching people (mostly strangers) and seeking knowledgeable individuals by referral to discuss with. This method was rigorous and discouraged people from undertaking the task of starting a business while some simply skipped the research and went straight to business believing they would learn the necessary things as they go (this produced mixed results with some succeeding and some failing).

Thankfully though, the internet has put an end to gruelling business research. Market survey and research today is much simpler. With a combination of self-curiosity and determination, together with knowing what questions to ask a search engine query, proper note taking skills, and the ability to self-educate and read in between the lines to form your own educated opinions, you can launch a research. A simple Google search engine research will compile books, journals, articles, videos, pictures as well as audio recordings, related to your search query (that are existent on the open web at that point in time) all in one place. The key to discovering the right results however is to understand the keywords in your questions. In other words, your search query will determine the type and amount of resources that will be returned to you by the search engine. Note that search engines have specific algorithms that could assist your research and increase productivity. Try to educate yourself on some of these tricks to make your research easier.

• **ADVERTISING AND MARKETING:** In the early days of our fathers, advertisements were generally passive. An advert then was simply a jingle on the radio or television, a column or page in a newspaper or magazine, posters, handbills, sign posts or word of mouth. Following the advent of the internet, more advertising options have come to the fore. Adverts are now more dynamic, active and invasive, thanks to the internet. This is further encouraged by the massive number of people on various social media platforms.

Businesses now bombard potential customers with numerous adverts (some subtle, some outrageous, and some in-between) daily in a bid to etch their brand, products and services deep into the subconscious of individuals to secure their loyalty. For the first time ever, digital ad spending in 2017 overshot television ad spending; while online ad spending reached $209 billion, television ad raked in $178 billion. At the rate which online ad is growing, Magna, the research arm of IPG Media brands forecasts that by 2050, online ad will make up 50% of all ad spending.

Marketing also has taken a huge boost from the internet. For instance, you no longer need to accost strangers on the street to take surveys. Now, you can simply draft your survey using one of the numerous survey sites and circulate the link on social media. This affords you a wider coverage at a significantly lesser cost and effort.

The impact of the internet has gotten to the point that any reasonable, well thought-out marketing campaign has to start on social media or at least take social media into consideration for it to have a noticeable effect.

Even for the slackers, now there is no excuse as to why you cannot promote your business, because with well-made promotional materials and little ad spend on social media marketing or influence marketing, you can advertise your business to the millions of individuals who are connected to the internet globally every single day.

• **ACCESS TO RESOURCES:** The internet allows billions of people using smartphones and computers around the world access to each other. There are roughly 30 zettabytes of data available on the internet with 12.6 billion online users adding content to the World Wide Web every hour and expanding. The global e commerce channel worldwide is expanding and is projected to reach roughly 4.4 trillion U.S dollars by 2020.

In 2016, I visited the beautiful island of Palawan in the Philippines. During our trek through the paradise, I was told by the locals that it was the first year they had received 24-hour electricity. Would you also believe that it had been the first time they were able to access the internet? 3G towers were built on the island, giving technological advances and even bypassing the era of landline infrastructures. It was amazing to see that the locals went from being in the dark to being able to access the internet which provides so much opportunity. Every day, the World Wide Web user base expands, thereby shortening the gap of distance and time between countries.

• **BUSINESS START-UP:** In times past, starting a business was a daunting task that required considerable mettle and clout. This was due to the amount of capital required, the rigorous processes to get the business registered as well as poor accessibility to necessary information. Through the internet however, social media marketing can be less expensive and more effective if used tactically. For example, if your product spreads quickly on social media through the use of memes or videos, it can be an effective way to gain notice of millions of people indirectly, which can create awareness of your brand or product... This can ultimately convert to sales. Many government sites, and third-party vendors can assist with research on how to incorporate your business. Information is readily and freely accessible with just the tap of a few buttons. The business registration procedure has also been made less tedious and searching your municipal website can provide you all you need in terms of application processes and local laws. All these have significantly reduced start-up costs and workload.

Your business could just start with a small low-cost website and advertising could be done at a low price via social media, blogs and news sites. With a website and the right type of online exposure, your business will be official to the public and the professionalism you've exuded will give you better leverage towards success.

- **PRODUCTIVITY:** In light of the above stated, it is reasonable to expect that the internet would have positive or negative impacts on the productivity of businesses. In the age of the internet, a business that does not incorporate the internet into its activities will be more likely to fail. A careful observation of a business that actively incorporates the internet into its operations as opposed to one that doesn't will instantly reveal that the one that actively incorporates the internet into its affairs is able to generate more value for its capital (i.e. is more productive), than the one that doesn't. This is largely due to the fact that many internet services (including those referred to above) are free to use (at least on a basic level), and where you do have to pay, it will most likely cost less than if you were to use the same service physically. So, that is less input for more output. The internet will allow your business to expand its footprint outside the brick and mortar storefront, allowing you to access more potential clientele at a greater distance. Think of it as a virtual storefront per say, where you have the means to direct foot traffic past your location.

However, the internet also has its downsides, it simply follows the trend where the purpose of a thing intended to be used for good is perverted by unscrupulous individuals. Thus, one has to be cautious about public image, in that some individuals will purposefully twist your words or actions out of context and blow events out of proportion due to the number of viewers or followers those individuals may have, causing bias through the strength of numbers.

The internet also levels the playing field to all who have access; this, in actuality, gives a business's clientele greater advantage in that the quality of service and products becomes highly competitive. All in all, the overall benefits far outweigh any disadvantages.

CHAPTER THREE

WHY YOU SHOULD INCORPORATE YOUR BUSINESS INSTEAD OF BUYING YOUR FAVOURITE SHOES

Now that you've started your business, and everything is going great, then what next? Finally buy that high-end shoe you've been dreaming of? Have you thought about incorporating your business? You haven't? Well you should.

First of all, what does it mean to incorporate a business? To incorporate a business is to set it apart as a separate legal entity from its owner. In other words, as far as the law and government is concerned, a corporation is capable of standing in its own right and with its own name without being joined to its owner. A corporation can sue and be sued in its own name, enjoys rights provided by the state it is domiciled, and its properties can be separate from that of its owner.

If you're incorporating your business in the US, do note that there are a few available options with various benefits including liability and tax advantages. Some examples of variations are a Corporation, Limited Liability Company, Professional Limited Liability Company, Partnership or even Sole Proprietorship. The needs of your business will determine which one of these options will better meet your needs. Simple research can help assist you in your decision and if you feel you need professional consultation, you can also consult with an attorney or accountant.

In the case of private limited companies, shares are not traded publicly but are assigned only amongst private individuals. The Corporate Affairs Commission however, allows for reregistration of a private company as a public company if the need arises.

On the other hand, shares of public companies are available for sale to the general public. Its shares are usually openly traded on the floor of the stock exchange. As to the benefits of incorporation, they greatly outweigh the identified disadvantages. Sadly, these benefits are not available in sole proprietorships and general partnerships.

- **Limited Liability**

This is the first and perhaps most important advantage of business incorporation. In sole proprietorships or partnerships, the business owner or the partners, as the case may be, are totally liable and responsible for the business' obligations. In other words, they are in the position to indemnify the business against debt, cost awarded against the business in judgement, etc. This means that creditors can go as far as pursuing the business owner's or the partner's personal properties to settle the business' debt. This approach is made possible by the fact that the law believes that unless a business is incorporated, the business and its owner or owners are one and the same.

After a business is incorporated however, the owner's liability is limited to the amount of shares they hold in the company. Furthermore, the business' creditors cannot go after the owner's personal property if the company is unable to pay its debt.

- **Continuity**

As stated above, as far as the law is concerned, an incorporated company has its own legal identity, separate from that of its owner. As such, it can enter into contracts, buy and own property, can sue and be sued in its own name. This implies that such a business can exist without the support of its owner and can outlive its directors.

This perpetuity in an incorporated business' life span makes it such that investors are more confident to commit their money to the company as opposed to committing such to a person as in the case of a sole proprietorship.

Once incorporated, a business' life span can only be brought to an end by a formal winding up, liquidation or by an order of the court. This implies that an incorporated business is in a better position to cater for the future generations of the owner's lineage. As such, it is a better legacy to leave for your children compared to a sole proprietorship which dies with you. If Henry Ford had not incorporated his business, Edsel Ford II would most likely not today be a member of the board of directors of Ford Motor Company.

- **Tax Reliefs**

Contrary to what most people think, an incorporated business is a more viable option for lower tax payments especially with proper accounting. This is because there are a couple of tax reliefs offered by the government in most countries meant to stimulate a greater interest in corporations by its citizens. These tax reliefs and rebates will certainly make life better (even if it is just by a little margin for the prudent company).

- **Credibility**

Due to the ease at which sole proprietorships and partnerships are formed, and also due to the fact that these business systems do not usually emphasise accountability, a business is not usually considered credible enough until it is incorporated. This position is further engendered by the fact that incorporations carry the force of the law to a greater degree than sole proprietorships.

The amount of trust people can place in the stability, credibility and constancy of a business to a large extent determines how willing they would be to transact with the business. Incorporation is generally considered a good indicator of this much sought-after credibility.

- **Generating Capital**

There are two broad methods of generating capital for a business and they are '**Equity**' and '**Debt**'. In a sole proprietorship, the only way business owners can raise capital is to dip hands into their personal resources or rely on contributions from family, friends and other well-wishers. In an incorporated business however, raising capital via equity involves issuing new shares of the company to the general public in exchange for some stake in the company.

As for debt financing, sole proprietorships, partnerships and corporations raise capital similarly. The process involves lending some amount of capital with the agreement to pay back with some predetermined appreciation rate at stipulated intervals. The difference however is that in the case of the sole proprietorships and partnerships, the owner(s) are personally responsible for the debt. Thus, if there is a default in repayment, the creditor can take over the owner's personal properties to clear the debt. In the case of a corporation however, the directors are not responsible for the company's debts except where they guarantee the debt. The company's assets will be used to repay such debts.

Obviously, an incorporated business provides safer options for generating capital as well as enjoys greater opportunities for investment, thus fostering a faster growth rate.

- **Sale**

As much as a business is oftentimes of great sentimental value to its owner, occasions do arise where you may decide it is time to let go of the business for one reason or the other, and herein lies another major advantage for incorporated businesses as opposed to sole proprietorships or a partnership.

Starting from getting a buyer, sole proprietorships and partnerships are generally less desirable to buyers. Incorporated businesses are much desirable for reasons of stability. Moreover, a change in ownership would not have a pronounced impact on the business as the business stands on its own.

While starting a business is all good and well, it is simply not enough to have it in the same state perpetually. It's important that you make efforts to scale up your business. Practice deferred gratification and do not lavish all the profit you make on luxuries.

While the opportunity to live a good life is one of the reasons for starting a business, you need to exercise patience so as not to kill your golden egg laying goose before it reaches maturity. So, in the context of this chapter's title, incorporate your business and let the shoes wait.

Furthermore, in times past, the process of incorporating a business used be tedious. Locating a lawyer, or some other necessary professionals, paying their fees, furnishing them with the necessary details, paying all required sums of money to the Corporate Affairs Commission (CAC), and waiting while hoping you don't get defrauded by the agent can put one under much financial and emotional strain. Today however, things have taken a turn for the better as more government services are being modified to ensure ease and speed of access.

In incorporating a business these days, it is possible for you to do away with an agent and do it yourself. The detailed procedure for incorporating a business is available online on different sites. All you have to do is fire up your search engine and search.

To take things a notch higher, many companies online such as Biz filings, Rocket Lawyer, and Legal Zoon will assist in incorporation process, making it simple and as straightforward without the need to visit an attorney or an accountant, who may charge you triple the amount. This will eliminate the need to travel anywhere physically because all of the documents submitted online, once approved, will be sent to you via email or regular way mail.

Now, you have no excuse for not incorporating your business to enjoy the cover that an incorporated business provides. With the same amount of money spent on frivolous materialistic items or less, you can legitimize your business.

CHAPTER FOUR

BUSINESS INSURANCE - YOUR PEACE OF MIND

Now imagine this – you have built a business and you that enjoys patronage from far and wide. Then one bright sunny morning, as you prepare for the day's work, you get a call from one of your business partners or employees who is talking so fast and sounding incoherent. You finally manage to calm him down enough for you to hear him say that on arriving at the business premises early that morning, he found your business premises being razed by fire.

The situation described above is precisely what happened to Adrian Furstenburg, a South African handbag designer on the cold winter morning of June 6, 2012. Adrian and his partner Nkululeko Msibi just landed a massive business order and had spent several hours and tons of money trying to pull off an impressive production. Unbeknownst to them however, a great disaster that would markedly affect the course of their business lives lurked around the corner.

Adrian was at a supplier's premises, picking up materials on that fateful Wednesday morning when he got a distress call from his partner, Mbisi. The only audible word he could pick from the call was "fire." He left everything he was doing and hurried off to the production studio. On getting there, what he saw was a cloud of smoke smouldering from the fire that had razed the entire production studio to the ground and turned their stock and items of equipment to a heap of rust and ashes. The most unfortunate part is that the business was not insured, so both partners lost all their investment and one of their biggest clients.

While the above-painted scenario is a nightmare that all reasonable business owners dread, it should come as no surprise to you that this happens more often than you think. For instance, in the US in 2016, 1 in 3 small businesses faced top hazards. All activities are prone to one kind of risk or another. Even Bill Gates agreed to that fact when he said, *"Business is a money game with few rules and a lot of risks."*

Business assets are lost daily to natural disasters, human error, theft, etc. and often, they cannot be recovered. There is, however, a remedy to these common concerns that can bring businesses to their knees and that is insurance.

To start with, what exactly is insurance? Insurance is a kind of contract established between an individual and an insurance company which empowers an individual to receive financial protection in the event of a contingent loss. So, the insured pays the insurer an amount of money (premium) at stipulated intervals in return for indemnity in the case of a failure which may include damage to the insured's property or the property of a third party, theft, injury, etc.

Now to be specific, business insurance is designed to protect businesses from unforeseen situations that may lead to a loss in the course of business. Enterprises evaluate their insurance needs based on the industries they operate and the kind of environment where they serve. The potential risks that companies generally face include; employee health and safety, legal liability, property damage or theft. Fortunately, there is an insurance cover for each kind of business risk.

As a registered Insurance Brokerage owner myself, I can outline 101 benefits that your business stand to enjoy if insured but I will only describe a few for lack of space and time, and they are as follows:

1) **Protection in the event of commercial litigation:** Whether we like it or not, conflict is a sure reality of business existence. Now imagine that a disgruntled employee sues your business, or you default on a contract, and the other party decides to seek redress in court. You get to court, your firm is found guilty, and the court orders you to pay a

considerable sum of money to the disgruntled party which is more than the value of the entire business. If your business insurance covers this scope of the incident, good for you but if not, your whole business could fold up. Examples abound of the companies that have filed for bankruptcy as a result of legal action. Just one breached contract, one slighted employee or one unsatisfied customer is enough to push you out of business if you do not have insurance.

2) **<u>Mitigate the risk of natural disaster</u>:** The planet more than ever has become more prone to natural disasters as a result of climate change. Floods, earthquakes, hurricanes, earth tremors and wildfires will not ask your permission before they strike. Estimates put the global economic loss associated with natural disasters in 2017 at \$175 billion. So, to make your bounce back after a natural disaster less strenuous and less financially draining, consider insuring your business against the risks of natural disasters.

3)   **<u>Enhances trust and credibility:</u>** Having insurance shows that your business has credibility, can be trusted and is bankable. If you want banks, investors, business partners, prospective clients (especially big corporations and government) to take your business seriously, then you need to have insurance cover. No right-thinking investor, (individual, corporate or lending organization) will knowingly put their money in a business that is uninsured and extremely prone to loss. Investors and lenders want to be sure that their interest will not be dangerously affected in the event of any unforeseen catastrophe. Some corporate organizations, government parastatals, and lenders will not go into business with you if your company doesn't have the required insurance covers.

4)   **<u>Boosts employee morale:</u>** In the words of Richard Branson, *"Your employees are your company's real competitive advantage. They are the ones making the magic happen – so long as their needs are being met."* One of the most significant needs of your

employees is the assurance that they are protected in the event of an accident while in the line of duty. Employees whose health and lives are insured will not hesitate to go the extra mile for your business. Moreover, as you protect your employees against hazard, you are invariably saving yourself from possible litigation especially if your company operates in high risk industries like construction, manufacturing, haulage, oil and gas, mining and agriculture where employees are at risk of disease, injury or even death. Also, providing insurance cover for your employees show that they are valued, and this will, in turn, help your business retain valuable employees and attract new talent.

5)   **<u>It is the law:</u>** Do you know that in some countries like the United States, Canada and Europe, businesses that have employees are legally bound to have certain types of insurance cover? In such countries, if your company has employees and you have no basic insurance requirements like employee disability, health insurance or workers' compensation,

your business may be fined, and you may face severe legal and civil consequences.

With the potential benefits of business insurance highlighted above, is it not surprising that 75% of American businesses are underinsured while 40% of small businesses have no form of protection at all? No wonder many small businesses do not survive their first challenge and many established enterprises fold up once they encounter the slightest difficulty. If your company has the right insurance covers, you can rest assured that the business to a large extent can weather any storm and come out of turbulent situations unscathed.

Insurance is always a wise business move that can hedge and mitigate risk, and there are different types of insurance cover for businesses that can be more or less risky. Some of the most important ones are here listed:

1) <u>**Workers' compensation insurance:**</u> In many countries across the globe, once a business employs

the first employee, workers' compensation insurance becomes a compulsion and penalties for non-compliance are often very strict. This type of insurance cover is meant to provide wage replacement, medical treatment, death and disability benefits to employees who suffer injury or meet their death while in the employ of your business. In the event that any of your employees has an accident, this kind of cover will cover the cost of their treatment, pay them while they are convalescing and in the extreme event of death, some form of compensation will be paid to their family. Besides, once your business puts this insurance cover up, the rights of employees to sue your firm in the event of any of the incidents covered by the workers' compensation insurance policy ceases to exist.

2) **<u>Professional liability insurance</u>:** I am quite sure you are very familiar with the famous aphorism, "no one is above mistake." Since we are talking in business context, let me put it as "no business is above mistake." Due to unforeseen situations like equipment breakdown, a business may be unable to deliver to a

client as and when due. Sometimes, human negligence or system malfunction may compromise service quality and or delivery time. If such situation arises, your client or business partner may become irate and choose to take legal action against your business. If you have the "errors and omissions insurance" cover (another name for professional liability insurance), you are safe as this policy defends businesses from negligence claims that may arise due to mistake or breach of contract. If your company doesn't have this kind of cover, trust me, you are on your own, and this may spell an abrupt end of the road for your business.

3)	**<u>Business interruption insurance:</u>** In the event of a natural disaster or other catastrophic happenstances like flood or fire, business activities may be grounded to a halt especially in the case of businesses like stores, banks or manufacturing plants whose operations are tied mainly to physical spaces. Needless to say that once activities become grounded, business income may be affected. But for a business that has this type of cover, the policy will provide compensation for revenue lost during the period of business hibernation. Based on your premium payment history, this kind of insurance cover can provide reimbursement for profits, costs of moving to and from a temporary location, loan payments, and even employee wages.

4)   **Property insurance:** For businesses that own premises, manufacturing plant, items of equipment, tools, furniture, stock and inventory, property insurance is an essential type of insurance to consider. This coverage provides sustenance for business in the unfortunate case of theft, vandalism or fire.

5)   **Product liability insurance:** If your business manufactures or distributes products, you should know that a customer might incur unexpected damage or loss in the course of using the products that you make or distribute. And it will not be unusual for the affected customer(s) to name your business in a lawsuit. If this happens, product liability insurance will save your company from various claims and cover all

the costs you incur while defending your business and product in the law court thereby saving your business from financial and reputation loss.

6) **<u>Business/commercial vehicle insurance:</u>** Vehicle insurance is arguably the most common type of insurance policy and is compulsory in almost all parts of the world. If your business has official vehicles, delivery trucks or staff buses, they must be fully insured to protect the company from liability in cases of accident or damage. If your business has commercial vehicle insurance, the insurer is obliged to pay you compensation to cover the cost of repair or replacement in the event of an accident, theft, vandalism and fire.

As mentioned earlier, all businesses are prone to contingent risks, and one of the best and perfect ways of addressing these risks is insurance. To save your company from unexpected failure and save yourself from bankruptcy, health failure or even untimely death that unforeseen business risks portend, get your business insured.

Before you start that business of yours or if you are in business already and do not have insurance, talk to an insurer today to know the specific kinds of insurance cover that your business requires; for instance, a one-person plumbing enterprise has no business procuring workers' compensation insurance and not all companies need product liability insurance.

However, there is a caveat that I would like to sound. In the course of procuring insurance, make sure to get insurance the right way by engaging registered insurance brokers, companies and agents. Moreover, in the case of any incidence that requires an insurance claim, make sure you keep records like pictures to use as evidence.

Insurance is meant to give you peace of mind so do not compromise that peace of mind by procuring fake business insurance. Get insured, rest assured!

Having touched on the importance of ensuring your business risks, let us go on to examine the other foundational necessities that you need to consider as you lay the foundations of your enterprise.

The Foundation of Starting and Scaling a Business

According to Small Business Administration (SBA), 95% of businesses fail within their first five years of existence. From my research and conversations with tens of business owners and advisors, I realized that business failure stems more often than not from improper planning, insufficient capital and lack of managerial experience. Other causes might include uncontrolled growth, overconfidence, inability to comply with government regulations, poor accounts management, not incorporating early, misapplication of business funds, lack of market understanding, etc.

I'm not trying to scare you right now. You don't have to be scared of starting a business because of the statistics and reasons for business failure I mentioned above. Trust me; your business can be one of the top 5% that will scale through the first five years and even much stronger if you plan well and seek professional counsel every step of the way.

The best advice I can provide, which is guaranteed to alleviate the loss of time and money, and to kick-start the establishment of business processes, is to get yourself a successful mentor.

CONSIDER MENTORSHIP

In the words of John C. Maxwell, *"One of the greatest values of mentors is the ability to see ahead what others cannot see and to help them navigate a course to their destination."*

You would agree with me that starting a business without much experience and little support is like groping in the dark. Guess you know what might happen when you fumble through the dark; you might miss a step, fall and crash down the stairs, you might hit your head against the wall, or walk right into a gaping hole. However, if there is someone who has the light of business mastery and is ready to guide you through the dark, you will most likely get out of that darkness unhurt.

While starting a business without much experience and little support is like groping in the dark, a successful mentor, on the other hand, can be likened to a torchbearer that can guide your feet from that darkness to the light of business success.

A successful mentor is someone that has walked the journey you set out to embark upon and has fought the many challenges that you will most likely encounter in your own journey. A successful mentor will give you candid advice and offer support (not necessarily financial) towards achieving positive outcomes in your business. A successful mentor can empower you and remarkably increase your chance of succeeding in business.

Besides, seeking out a mentor says a lot about who you are as a person. It shows you are teachable, open to the perspectives of others and adaptable to change.

You might say "why do I need a mentor when I can just type any question on google and get answers in an instant?" While that is true, I want you to know that experience has no substitute and you cannot pour your heart out to Google (and trust me, as you go through this entrepreneurial journey, there will be many days when the only thing you would crave is someone to unbundle your heart). On days when you turn to google but cannot find answers to your complex business challenge, a mentor can help you solve that knotty business problem by sharing their real-world experience to provide solutions that you could not find in the pages of a business textbook or by surfing the internet.

Moreover, as people who have been in business long before you, it is certain that your mentor will have extensive business and even government network that you can leverage if and when the need arises. In addition, if you are the kind of person that has challenges with keeping to commitments, plans, and timelines, having a mentor can help you be more accountable because a good mentor will see that you set realistic, achievable goals and hold you accountable to make sure you reach them at the set time. This sentiment of mine is succinctly put by Dylan Hrycyshen who said; "*A mentor relationship is about goal setting and action planning. A mentor should not be doing work for you. Set the expectations up front, make it known what you need help with and that your mentor has the skills or network to assist.*"

If you look around you and across the globe, you will realize that none of the greatest and most successful entrepreneurs in world history have reached where they are without the support of a mentor or mentors. Thomas A. Scott mentored Andrew Carnegie, Steve Jobs mentored Mark Zuckerberg, and Richard Branson said about his mentor, "*It's always good to have a helping hand at the start. I wouldn't have got anywhere in the airline industry without the mentorship of Sir Freddie Laker.*"

In fact, according to a survey conducted by Sage, 93% of the business owners polled agreed that mentorship is a critical success factor in business. Another executive coaching survey conducted by Stanford University revealed that 80% of CEOs who took part in that survey had received some form of mentorship at different times in their career.

Now let 's talk about how to spot a good mentor and how to establish a relationship with them.

FINDING A SUCCESSFUL MENTOR

The first thing I will tell you in your quest to get a mentor is, "avoid Generals who have no scars", i.e., avoid people who seem to have it too easy in business. Business owners that have not faced any serious challenges in their business. My reason for saying this should be quite apparent; if the supposed person has not had to deal with some challenging business situation, how can they possibly help you when you face one in your own business.

Secondly, if you are going to get a mentor, look for someone who plays in the industry where you operate or plan to work. Remember, Mark Zuckerberg's mentor was not Michael Bloomberg, but Steve Jobs, and Richard Branson's mentor was Sir Freddie Laker, not Warren Buffett. Mentors who play in the same industry as you have more knowledge about the industry, have seen it all in that industry, have surmounted the challenges that are peculiar to that industry and are in a better position to give you relevant, applicable advice when you face similar issues.

However, you should note that getting the attention of and convincing successful entrepreneurs to mentor you may be a daunting task as their schedules are packed. So get a way to do something generous for them to get their attention. You can as well explore online or offline methods of connecting with them. You can send them an email, connect with them on social media, go to their favorite relaxation spot, attend an event where they would be at. If all these doesn't work, explore your current network to see if there's anyone who has a personal relationship with them and ask that they introduce you. When you finally get an appointment with them, make sure you go prepared. Listen attentively to what they say, do not be too demanding and ask intelligent questions.

HIRE A LAWYER

When I say you need a lawyer for your business, I am not talking the Harvey Specter or Mickey Haller type; lawyers who go to settle legal scores in front of a judge and present their clients with massive bills. When I say your small business needs a lawyer, I mean you need a transactional lawyer and not a litigator.

Who is a transactional lawyer you might ask? A transactional lawyer exists and works to help you get the most value for your business. Unlike litigators who save you in court, an excellent transactional lawyer works to ensure that you and your business don't get to court in the first instance. They help you understand the legal implications and perspectives of your business transactions and give you strategic advice in that wise.

A business lawyer will ensure that all aspects of the business function well. They can help you secure trademark protection for your brand, patent your inventions, get better terms from your business partners, draft substantial contracts, interview and hire employees and also deal with governmental regulation issues amongst many other things.

Such a lawyer will come to your rescue if you happen to find your business enmeshed in environmental issues or one of your employees wakes up one day and decides to sue you on some flimsy ground. Moreover, they will advise you on how best to deal if your competitor copies your invention or your business partners try to short-change you.

If you decide to sell the business, merge with a bigger one or want to acquire another, they protect your interests and help you get the best deals.

As your lawyer grows with the business and becomes more acquainted with how it runs, they can even help you spot long and short-term opportunities for growth and expansion.

Consider a consulting arrangement with a transactional lawyer and include the cost in your business plan. If you wait till your business needs a lawyer before you get one, then you might be setting your company up for failure as this kind of approach might turn out to be outrageously expensive and downright deadly. I'm sure you remember what they say about prevention being better than cure.

LET AN ACCOUNTANT MANAGE YOUR BOOKS

In trying to cut costs and maximize profits, many business owners, especially at the start-up phase fail to see any need for hiring an accountant to manage their company's books. By doing their tax, audit and business accounts themselves, many business owners have run into financial straits. Before I go further, I would like to share some statistics with you.

Small Businesses and Accountants Depend On Each Other

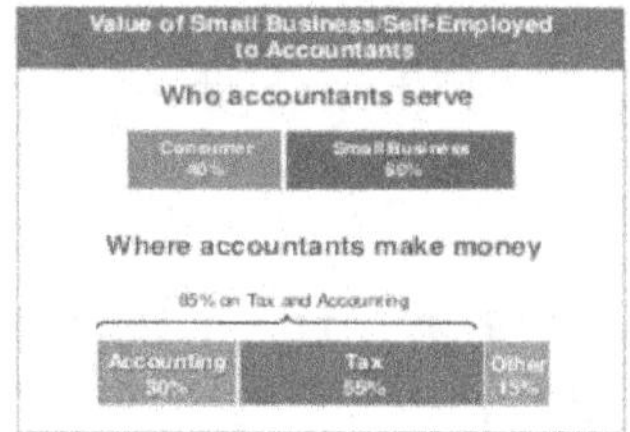

Need I say more with this result from a survey conducted by Intuit? After all, a picture they say is worth more than a thousand words.

Without mincing words, every business needs the usual advice of an accountant right from the start-up stage. First, conferring with an accountant while you are in the process of setting up your business can help you determine which kind of legal structure is best for your type of business and industry while also assisting you to open the right kind of company account that will set your business on the right financial footing.

As your revenue increases, so does your tax. However, you may not know and might likely end up underpaying tax. Meeting regularly with an accountant will save you from embarrassment by ensuring that you do not fall into the tax underpayment net. In the same vein, if your business will involve some level of export, handling the sales tax issue by yourself may be an uphill task.

Besides, an accountant can help you oversee your inventory, company payroll, and payment processes. When the time comes for you to deal with the government, an accountant is best at compiling and submitting the necessary paperwork to relevant agencies, creating your annual financial report and doing tax calculations on your behalf. If you form a partnership or one partner leaves or another one joins, you need the help of an accountant to organize and record share and stock allocation.

Furthermore, as your business grows, accountants can assist you to raise capital for expansion, help you determine areas for growth by providing insight on cash flow patterns, offer advice on property acquisition or leasing and create financial forecasts that will help you make better decisions in your business. You can use their tax planning expertise as well to legally reduce tax liabilities.

In the same vein, while the internet has made it quite easy for entrepreneurs to set up accounting software themselves, you still need the help of an accountant to help you chart it appropriately and set it up so that it works effectively.

Trust me, there are a thousand ways that your business will be better if you seek the consult of a dexterous accountant right from when you start your business. I am very well aware that you might be a start-up that cannot afford to employ an in-house accountant just yet. To reduce the expense, you can choose to outsource an accountant to help you set up each phase of your financial growth process. You can decide to use a combined approach where you do the groundwork and get the accountant to help you look through and give advice as fit.

All the same, the major crux of the matter is that you need to let an accountant manage your financial issues for you if you want your business to avoid unnecessary financial mishaps and grow to become more profitable than it currently is.

CHAPTER FIVE

BROADENING YOUR COMFORT ZONE SUCCESSFULLY

A comfort zone is a physical space or emotional state that makes you feel safe, secure and comfortable. In your comfort zone, you have a vast sense of certainty; things are very familiar and pretty much predictable. Things are so easy and effortless to the extent that they do not require you to exert extra effort. In your comfort zone, there's nothing new to learn, no new skill to acquire and no challenging task to tackle as you have already mastered everything that is required to live in that zone. While that zone feels so cozy and comfortable, it is, however, a dangerous place to be for it is the breeding ground for complacency which in turn begets mediocrity.

It's only by doing new and unfamiliar things that we grow and innovate. By doing things the same way, following the same method and routine, we remain the same. But by doing the things that scare us, going higher to expand our learning curves, we grow more confident, and it is that confidence that spurs us to push beyond the limits of what is deemed possible.

Below are some of the actions that will help you escape the indulgent trappings of your comfort zone:

Imbibe the habit of journaling: Get a journal and start writing in it the perceived boundaries of your comfort zone. Write down the things that scare you or make you feel uncomfortable; it might be cold calling, public speaking or networking. It is human to have vulnerabilities, and the first step in turning our vulnerabilities to strength is to first acknowledge them. Think about your weaknesses, write them down and write down the daily actions you would take to overstep those boundaries every day.

Meeting new people is always an opportunity to learn new things and also a confidence-booster. Attend more events, go to the library, join a new group in your community or attend a business seminar where you can exchange ideas on diverse range of topics with other people. Iron, they say, sharpens iron. So, by meeting people and exchanging ideas with them, you gain new perspectives on how to do things better in your business.

For some people, like Richard Branson, you can as well **pursue adrenaline pumping adventures**. Go sky-diving with a bunch of friends; learn how to swim; try mountaineering; travel the world on a scooter or in a hot balloon. You can even decide to travel to space. When you embark on scary adventures like this, you unconsciously become increasingly empowered to take bolder steps in your business that will translate to more success.

Having a hobby can help you maintain balance, ease stress and teach you creative and problem-solving skills which can have powerful ripple effects on your business. For instance, if your hobby is photography, you will continuously have many creative decisions to make when trying to get beautiful shots. When you hold a camera, questions like "From what angle should I take this shot? Is the lighting enough? Does this background blend?" will crop up in your head. And trust me, being able to solve problems in such a creative way will help you build the mental muscle to solve more problems and make better decisions in business. Besides, cultivating a hobby is good for brain development and helps prevent Alzheimer's disease.

Also, **cultivate the habit of reading**. Reading takes you to places you have never been, shows you situations that you might have never known about your business and the world around you. Do not stick to things that you find interesting to read or to business books alone. Read all sorts of things because as an entrepreneur, the challenges that you would face every day are such that will require a dynamic kind of approach. Follow local and international news, read novels and sports magazines, study philosophy and read fashion blogs. Read things that your friends, colleagues and family members would not believe you are reading; comics, cookbooks or travel guides.

Many people resist the urge to leave their comfort zones because it is a very comfortable place to be. Getting out of your comfort zone takes a lot of gut and requires a high dose of mental toughness. However, you can make your journey into the uncomfortable terrain beyond your comfort zone easier by beginning with small changes. You don't need to start by flying. You can start by crawling. Just make sure you take small steps to move outside your comfort zone daily. As they say, life begins at the end of your comfort zone.

"Move out of your comfort zone. You can only grow if you are willing to feel awkward and uncomfortable when you try something new." - **Brian Tracy**

Note that as you move out of your comfort zone to realize your goals, you start to get comfortable again in the new area after a while. After you have pulled and pushed to get a new version of your product out there and it has been accepted, you tend to take things slower and relax a bit. To therefore continue growing and not fall into complacency, you need to push yourself into new levels of discomfort continually. You must continue to innovate in business, think up new products or look for ways to make your services better. The most successful entrepreneurs never allow themselves to get comfortable. Think of Richard Branson who is continually innovating his business and even pushing himself beyond limits by doing scary things; things that endanger his life (now I'm not saying you should threaten your life).

If Steve Jobs had remained in the comfort zone of just making computers, we would today not have iPods, iPads or iPhones. If Henry Ford had stayed in his comfort zone, maybe we would still be riding carts. What about the Wright brothers? If they had not pushed the boundaries of their limit, perhaps, air travel would still remain a quixotic mirage. Elon Musk got out of his comfort zone when he left PayPal to start Tesla. Taraji P. Henson moved out of her comfort zone when she decided to move to the uncertain terrain of California with her son. Imagine if Dr. Martin Luther King (Jr.) had opted to remain in his comfort zone.

Are the people mentioned above better or worse for it by stepping out of their comfort zones? You need to realize that success as an entrepreneur is not a destination, it is a journey, and you must be on your toes always, anticipating your customers' needs and looking for best ways to meet those needs. It is by leaving your comfort zone that you can change your own life and become a blessing to the entire world.

You must, however, note that it can get cold, lonely and difficult outside your comfort zone. Challenges that you may never have confronted before will come up, and more situations will arise that require courage and endurance. Most of the goals that you have yet to reach in your entrepreneurship journey lie outside your comfort zone, and each target has a set of challenges attached to it. Each of these barriers are the hurdles standing between you and your dreams. If you, therefore, refuse to confront each with confidence and tenacity, your goals will most likely remain dreams.

USING EDUCATION TO TAKE CALCULATED RISKS IN BUSINESS

The debate on whether formal education provides the necessary grounding for entrepreneurship and whether practice is the only route to entrepreneurial success has been raging for many years. Others even hold the opinion that entrepreneurs are born and not made; that entrepreneurs have certain traits which set them apart from other people.

When talking about the needlessness of formal education to entrepreneurship, many are quick to point out that a number of the most successful entrepreneurs in the world today are famous for being college dropouts while some did not even attend college at all. Mark Zuckerberg, Richard Branson, Steve

Jobs, Bill Gates, Larry Ellison, Michael Dell, John Mackey, Rachel Ray, Kevin Rose are favourite examples.

From MIT to the University of Pennsylvania or Makerere University, lecturers, professors and teachers of business abound. Their academic qualifications do not necessarily qualify them to be entrepreneurs because to be candid, possessing vast knowledge about business necessarily does not translate to business success. You are only qualified to use the tag entrepreneur if you are a business owner whose livelihood and sustenance depends on risk taking, innovation and creation.

Without mincing words, there are certain circumstances when it is better to seek knowledge in a structured setting. Such an instance is if you want to gain profound insights into a particular field of business endeavour. For example, courses in marketing, accounting, law, business administration, and project management will be beneficial and come in handy throughout your entrepreneurial lifespan. While academic education might not be convenient or liberal enough for everyone, there are times when knowledge acquired from formal training can be useful.

It is quite understandable if you choose not to pursue the route of formal education route; it is surely not a prerequisite to business success. It can, however, make your entrepreneurial journey easier in the long run. Various studies have established the fact that education is of immense benefits in an entrepreneur's journey. One of such studies is the Global Entrepreneurship Monitor (GEM) study of 2010 which suggests that there is a definite link between opportunity-driven entrepreneurship and level of education. Jiminez et al. (2015) also stated that education could foster entrepreneurial success in the sense that it increases self-esteem and boosts confidence levels hence reducing the perceived risks associated with starting a business.

By acquiring formal education, individuals can learn how to deal with and overcome failure, manage pressure and become adept at setting and meeting goals. Also, school can be a great place for building long lasting friendships and relationships that could foster your business connections in the distant or not so distant future. Even after college, being a member of your alumni association (especially if you attended a prestigious college) can open many doors of business opportunities and partnerships for you.

In another vein, while a college degree might not be so pivotal to success in one industry, it might be critical if you want to become an entrepreneur in some particular fields. While talking about his decision to complete his college education at Wharton University at a time when it is almost the norm not to have a college degree (especially in the field of technology), Daniel Fine, founder of Glass-U admitted that it could be severe and extremely challenging to make headway as an entrepreneur in sectors like medicine or finance without college education. The long and short of it is that education can boost your chances of success in business.

I must admit that it is crucial for entrepreneurs to expand their knowledge base and skill set by getting an education, this education may necessarily not be acquired within the perimeters of a college or university ground as there are many routes you can tow to get an education or expand your knowledge.

In essence, the truth is that there is no one right way about it; choose and pursue whichever works best for you. Whether you prefer formal education or decide to learn by doing, make sure that you learn the ground rules and understand the basics of building, operating and scaling a business. Furthermore, I believe education will only enhance knowledge, so unless your business is in creativity, education will help further your growth.

THE BENEFITS OF PROPER RESEARCH IN BUSINESS

You got a fantastic business idea! That's nice to hear. But before you go ahead with execution, I want to know how much research you have done about starting a business generally and what it takes to start a business in your particular area of interest?

Aaron Keller, Managing Principal of Capsule, says, "*It's a big red flag when someone outlines the size of the market - multibillion dollars - but doesn't clearly articulate a plan for how the idea will meet an unmet need in the marketplace.*" This statement vividly foregrounds the fact that between the ideation and execution stages is an essential stage which is the research stage.

Whether you are a serial entrepreneur or first-time business owner, the first thing to do when a new business idea pops in your head is to carry out proper, articulate research. You need to undertake primary and secondary research in the line of business you want to establish. I dare say that the viability and the success of your business hinge on how in-depth and meticulous your research is. It is through thorough investigation that you will assess the feasibility of your idea, the market segment, existing challenges in that segment, existing competition, potential opportunities, the effectiveness of sales, the purchasing power and prospective buying habit of your proposed customers, etc. With all these adequately done before you go into business, you reduce your chances of failure to the barest while increasing your success rate to a great extent.

Aaron Keller again puts it nicely by saying; *"The more you do before you launch, the less you'll have to do [afterward], and the less painful the lessons tend to be."*

Below, I highlight some of the most critical aspects of a business that you need to research before staking your savings on that business idea.

Business structure

You need to research the type of legal structure most appropriate for your kind of business as this will go a long way to determine how you will run the company and manage the finances.

Assess your competition(s)

To stay ahead of your game and grab a share of the market, you must know how your competitors conduct business, their strengths, and their weaknesses. You can as well learn from their mistakes to avoid similar errors in your own business.

Know your customers

Every business has a target audience as they say that "appealing to everyone is appealing to no one." To succeed in business, you have to map the kind of people your products and services would serve. Will you sell to millennials or baby boomers, male or female? You need to know the habits and temperament of your target customers before you can predict how to appeal to them and how best to serve them.

Write a business plan

Your business plan gives a holistic view of your business and proves the viability and feasibility of your business idea. It is the roadmap that will guide your business to success. It is what investors and bankers will base their investment and lending decisions on and therefore must be written with precision and much knowledge.

However, research is not limited to the start-up phase only. After you have launched your new enterprise and yonder, you must continue periodic research to note the loopholes in your plan and how to proffer lasting solutions to those challenges. Continuous research also helps you evaluate your progress against that of your competitors and provide insight into the strategies that you can device to beat your rivals. With research, you will stay on top of the market as you can effectively study the habits and attitudes of your existing and potential customers to anticipate their needs and meet those needs before anyone else.

If you have enough funds to spare, you can engage the services of professional business consultants to help you through the research process. However, if your budget is tight, you can undertake the process yourself with resources from the internet, entrepreneurial publications, local libraries, business journals, advice from mentors, etc.

CIRCLE OF INFLUENCE (YOUR NETWORK IS YOUR NET WORTH)

The process of ideas and information exchange among individuals or group of individuals that share similar interests and or ties is what I refer to as networking, and it may be for business or social purposes. For this book, however, I will dwell specifically on networking for business.

Place of work, social clubs, school, industry associations are examples of areas where people form business alliances. We have examples of many people who built business partnerships while in college; Daniel Ha and Jason Yan, Steve Huffman and Alexis Ohanian, Chude Jideonwo and Debola Williams, Jerry Yang and David Filo all met and built the foundations of their business partnerships either as undergraduates or graduate students in college.

Business networking helps individuals foster relationships that boost the prospects of business success regarding knowledge, skills or lead that can generate more revenue.

Networking is one of the essential business marketing tools for small businesses. As a small business owner with a tight marketing budget, you can use networking as leverage to reach and sell your business to a large number of people who operate within and beyond your industry. At networking events, you have unlimited access to a large pool of influential people who can give you your next lead. As more people know about your business, the number of your potential customers soar. Networking can also open vistas of new opportunities for partnerships, investment, or business expansion. Moreover, attending networking events can help build and maintain substantial reputation capital for you and your business. The more networking events you attend, the more your profile grows and trust me, it helps put your business brand and your own name in a right perception in the minds of the people that matter.

In the same light, networking can help you keep abreast of latest developments in your industry especially given the dynamic nature of business in this age. It is also an effective method of learning new things and gaining fresh ideas and insights that could help your business. When you attend networking events and converse with other people, you tap from their own peculiar experiences and knowledge. Some of the people you meet might even offer you unsolicited advice that could save you time, money and other vital resources.

Furthermore, I hope you know that it is no curse if I say that the early phase of starting your business will often be fraught with challenges. The good news, however, is that regular networking can be your assistance in these stormy days.

Above and beyond, entrepreneurs are known to possess high energy levels, a positive mind set and an optimistic approach to life. Regularly meeting and hobnobbing with them as individuals or in groups will surely boost your morale and do your confidence level a lot of good.

However, to be clear, networking goes beyond attending events to eat small chops and punch. It's more about connecting with people and establishing genuine relationships with them. To, therefore, make the most of your networking efforts, you must be intentional about the process. First, you should note that the most rewarding relationships whether in business or love are ones that are mutually beneficial. As you network in the industry, think more of what you can give first, not of what you stand to gain. Listen to people attentively and be more interested in how you can help them. Give as much information, support, and knowledge as you receive.

Secondly, the spread of your network does not matter as much as the substance and quality. Instead of joining six or seven mushroom business groups, be an active participant of two quality groups where you should put yourself forward by being an active participant.

Some of the business networking groups you can consider are; the Chamber of Commerce and Industry in your state, the local chapter of Rotary Club in your district or professional and trade associations that are in line with your business.

CHAPTER SIX

THE CRITICAL ESSENCE OF TIMING

You may not have heard it enough, or you may have heard but found it so hard to believe. But believe it or not, it remains an enduring truth that timing is one of the most critical factors that determine the success or failure of start-ups; much more important than execution.

Timing is so essential because it can markedly change the course of your business. If you have a great idea, best-in-class work ethic and a clear vision, your company might still not turn out good if you launch at a wrong time. I have heard many people equate timing with luck, but that necessarily is not the case. While I do not disapprove the fact that some stroke of luck and good fortune sometimes play out in business, timing in business is not hinged on chance per se because it takes a lot of work regarding quality study of market movement and dynamics, coupled with a meticulous study of customer psychology.

Simply put, timing in business relates to being smart enough to use your idea or product to fill a need or needs that are in present demand. It is necessarily a function of finding the right balance between demand and supply.

You must, however, note that the fact that a product or service is not in demand currently does not mean customers won't accept it. If you play the timing card well, armed with empirical research about market situation and customer mood, you can anticipate the needs of customers and make a fortune by selling to them, goods or services they had no prior idea that they needed until you introduce them – think of Steve Job's iPod; "a thousand songs in your pocket".

Do you know that one of the significant factors that led to the overwhelming success of Airbnb is timing?

Notwithstanding the fact that many investors refused to stake their money on the start-up because they thought no one (especially in times like this when crime and terrorism rate is on a high) would rent out their house to random strangers, the company has however grown to become one of the highest revenue grossers in the world. I can boldly state that Airbnb succeeded because they listened to the heartbeat of their customers and the sounds of the market before stepping out.

A couple of years ago, founder of IdeaLabs, Bill Gross carried out an extensive study of over a hundred businesses to find out the most critical success factors in entrepreneurship. The elements he put forward in his consideration are funding, business model, timing, idea and team. While making public the results of his study, Bill stated that 42 per cent of the difference between success and failure could be attributed to timing which makes timing the number one factor. Following closely at second place is execution and team while idea takes the number three spot. What

Bill's study tells us is that before going ahead full blaze with your plan, you need to study the attitude and habit of your prospective customers as well as market dictates first so that you won't be like the merchant who chose to sell raincoats in summer.

"Timing, perseverance and ten years of trying will eventually make you look like an overnight success." In the fore-stated quote, you can see that Biz Stone, co-founder of Twitter put timing even before perseverance and hard work and I do not believe that it's a mere coincidence. Even Warren Buffet is quoted to have quipped once that; "Time is the friend of the wonderful business, the enemy of the mediocre."

I'm quite sure you know what they say about being too early and being too late to the market. How will you know if you are too early or too late to the market if you don't even know anything about timing? For your idea to succeed, you need to understand the things that are within your control and the factors you have to monitor. You need to feel the pulse of your proposed industry to note how the present conditions in that industry could affect your product or service.

To put things in better perspective, let's examine two different hypothetical scenarios. First, we have John. John has a fabulous idea, a brilliant business model, surplus capital and a team composed of Harvard and MIT alums. However, John refused to study market trends and customer mood before launching. It turns out that the market was not ripe enough for his products offering. His great products flood the market, but sales were very slow because the product does not match the current needs of customers and only a few could afford the products owing to the recent economic downturn.

On the other hand, is Kate. Fresh out of college, Kate comes up with a reasonably good idea, scratches her savings and seeks financial help from family and friends to raise enough capital and convinces two of her former classmates to join her in the pursuit of her vision. But unlike John, Kate makes it a point to check the pulse of her proposed customers and the conditions of the industry she wants to play in. To her greatest surprise, she realises that the solution her company offers is the answer to one of the most significant gaps that other companies playing in that same industry have not paid considerable attention to. With her not so great business structure, Kate goes straight to business, hoping to grow her business as revenue and market share expands.

Going by the two hypothetical situations above, who do you think has a better prospect to succeed in business between John and Kate?

While John will lose a huge amount of money and a sizeable amount of his self-esteem, Kate will go ahead to use the revenue from her initial sales to flesh out her idea and hire a better team which will place her start-up on the pedestal of impressive growth.

As it is in the case of John and Kate, so it is in all businesses; timing can be what makes or breaks a company.

Sometimes you might be so passionate about the ingenuity of your idea that all you want to do is jump into action. Don't take a blind leap. Do not let your heart lead you astray. Take some time to really study your market and customers before you commit. Moreover, accept and own the results that you get, do not be in denial of the fact of your situation so you don't end up burning your fingers. The fact that the market is not ripe enough today or that your customers are not ready yet for your products does not mean things will not change. If you stay vigilant and smart, things will work in your favour when the time is right. And if you can't wait, try tweaking your idea a bit or work on another idea.

While it is almost impossible to have a picture-perfect market and customer readiness view, one can get close to accuracy by studying market trends and customer mood from past years. Some time-tested tools and methods can aid your research. One of such is the **Industry Structure Analysis** also known as the **Porter Five Forces Analysis** which was made famous by Professor Michael Porter of Harvard Business School. Professor Porter's method, which was initially published in his book titled **"Competitive Strategy: Techniques for Analysing Industries and Competitors"**, is used to analyse the intensity of competition and level of profitability in business industries. The five forces recognised by Porter are; competition in the industry, the threat of new entrants into the industry, the power of suppliers, the power of customers and risk of substitute products.

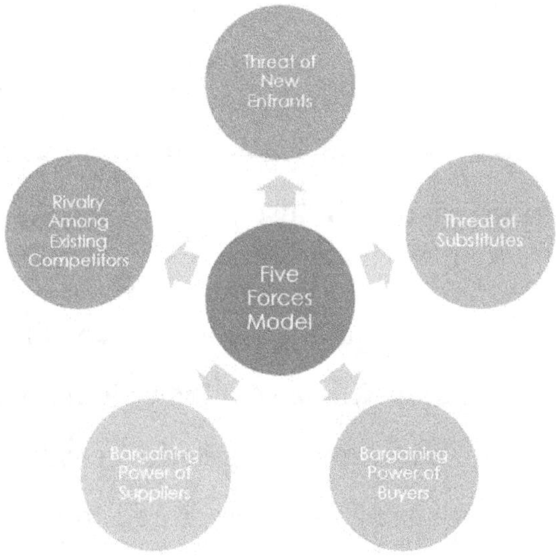

Competition in the industry: The level of competition among existing businesses in an industry goes a long way to determine how profitable the industry will be. In sectors where companies have to compete aggressively, profits may be low. If there are already many competing businesses in a particular sector and majority of companies playing in that industry are of equal size, it is quite easy for suppliers and customers to switch. However, in sectors where competition is low, companies will surely be able to gross higher revenue.

The threat of new entrants: The easier it is for competitors to enter a particular industry, the stiffer the competition in that industry would be. As more businesses compete for sales in the same market, the profit potential of that market will become slim. The threat of new entrants will be very high for an industry where; there is no government regulation, products are identical, the amount of capital required to enter the industry is low and businesses already playing in the industry do not have peculiar brand identities.

Power of suppliers: If there are few suppliers but many buyers or if raw materials are scarce and will cost a whopping sum for firms to switch suppliers, then suppliers hold dominant powers to affect the operations of businesses. The more you depend on suppliers, the more powerful they become because if they choose to drive up prices outrageously or sell materials of low quality to you, your profit margin and product quality will be compromised.

Power of customers: There isn't much difference between the power of customers and the power of suppliers. What the power of customers implies is that the smaller your customer base is or, the easier it is for them to switch to another firm, the more power they hold to drive down price.

The threat of substitute products: If buyers have a plethora of products to choose from that are of superior quality or lower price to yours, then the power of your business in that market can be weakened. For instance, you cannot compare the cost and ease of switching from Pepsi to Coca-Cola with the price and ease of changing from Toyota to Rolls Royce.

Besides, **The Change Factors Analysis** often referred to as **PESTEL Analysis** is also a very helpful tool as regards timing. The PESTEL analysis is a framework used to analyse and understand the macro-environmental forces (Political, Economic, Social, Technological, Environmental and Legal) that can influence and shape the performance of industries and organisations remarkably.

As an entrepreneur just starting a new venture or entering a foreign market, all the aspects covered by PESTEL analysis are what you should pay critical attention to no matter your industry. This analysis has become one of the essential tools of strategic management.

Some of the questions you have to keep in mind while conducting the PESTEL analysis include; What is the economic situation of the country? How charged is the political climate of the country and how does the present political reality affect your proposed industry (remember how Donald Trump's emergence as the president of America had specific effects on the American economy)? Are there technological innovations that can affect the market structure (think of artificial intelligence and big data)? What is the legislation regulating operations in the industry? Etc.

Political Factors: Political factors or forces relate to all the influences that government has in your proposed industry and to what level government intervenes in the economy. These factors may include tax policy, international trade policy, level of political stability, stance on corruption, labour laws and foreign policy, to mention a few.

Economic Factors: These are the factors that shape the performance of a country's economy. Such factors include foreign exchange rate, interest rate, inflation rate, unemployment rate, per capita income, gross domestic product, gross national income and so on. Economic factors will strongly influence how successful your start-up will be as they are the factors that determine the purchasing power of your potential customers and how you will price your products and services.

Social Factors: When we talk about social factors, we are concerned with the characteristic norms, culture and value that shape the attitude and behaviour of the populace. Factors such as security situation, population growth rate, age distribution, lifestyle, cultural beliefs, religiosity, value orientation and level of education goes a long way to determine how people will respond to your products and give you an idea of the things you need to consider while developing your marketing strategy.

Technological Factors: Being conversant with what goes on in your country's and the global technology space would help you make better production decisions. For instance, you will be able to determine which is more cost effective between self-producing and outsourcing production. Factors like level of technological advancement, speed of technological change, research and development activity will let you know the production technologies you should invest in and the ones you should avoid.

Having a grasp of how fast the technological landscape changes and how such changes can affect your business and industry will help you stay ahead of your competitors.

Environmental Factors: Now that subjects of climate change, greenhouse gas emission, environmental sustainability and global warming are at the forefront of business discussions globally, issues like source of raw materials and product ingredient now significantly influence the buying pattern of consumers. Growing awareness about environmental issues has remarkably changed the operational strategy and product offering of many ventures.

Legal Factors: Knowing the legal principles that affect the conduct of enterprises in your country of operation will save you from trouble and help your growth. Legal factors that you must consider include tax laws, employment and labour laws, copyright and patent laws, health and safety laws, international trade laws and consumer protection laws. You need to be aware of business conducts that are acceptable and those that are not acceptable in your industry for you to operate successfully.

Below is a comprehensive list of PESTEL factors that you should consider:

Political factors

- Government stability/instability
- Corruption level
- Tax policies
- Freedom of press
- Government regulation and deregulation
- Special tariffs
- Political action committees
- Government involvement in trade unions and agreements
- Competition regulation
- Voter participation rates
- Amount of government protests
- Defence expenditures
- Level of government subsidies
- Bilateral relationships
- Import-export regulation/restrictions
- Trade control
- Lobbying activities
- Size of government budgets

Economic factors

- Growth rate
- Interest rate
- Inflation rate
- Exchange rate
- Availability of credit
- Level of disposable income
- The propensity of people to spend
- Federal government budget deficits
- Gross domestic product trend
- Unemployment trend
- Stock market trends
- Price fluctuations

Social factors

- Population size and growth rate
- Birth rates
- Death rates
- Number of marriages
- Number of divorces
- Immigration and emigration rates
- Life expectancy rates

- Age distribution
- Wealth distribution
- Social classes
- Per capita income
- Family size and structure
- Lifestyles
- Health consciousness
- Average disposable income
- Attitude towards government
- Attitude towards work
- Buying habits
- Ethical concerns
- Cultural norms and values
- Sex roles and distribution
- Religion and beliefs
- Racial Equality
- Use of birth control
- Education level
- Minorities
- Crime levels
- Attitudes towards saving

- Attitude towards investing
- Attitudes towards retirement
- Attitudes toward leisure time
- Attitudes towards product quality
- Attitudes toward customer service
- Attitudes towards foreign people

Technological factors

- Technology incentives
- Automation
- R&D activity
- Technological change
- Access to new technology
- Level of innovation
- Technological awareness
- Internet infrastructure
- Communication infrastructure
- The life cycle of technology

Environmental factors

- Weather
- Climate
- Environmental policies

- Climate change

- Pressures from NGO's

- Natural disasters

- Air and water pollution

- Recycling standards

- Attitudes toward green products

- Support for renewable energy

Legal factors

- Discrimination laws

- Antitrust laws

- Employment laws

- Consumer protection laws

- Copyright and patent laws

- Health and safety laws

- Education laws

- Consumer protection laws

- Data protection laws

By taking advantage of tools such as Porter's Five Forces and PESTEL analyses to understand how fortuitous times are, you become empowered to see the present and have a good grasp of what the future portends for your business; valuable information that makes you better prepared to drive your idea to tremendous success.

However, before I close this chapter, let me state that apart from knowing the right time for you to launch, there are few personal questions you need to ask yourself. And answering these questions honestly will determine whether your business will be a great success or an epic failure.

To begin with, on a personal level, you must be able to tell how ready you are, how much time you can dedicate, how much technical expertise and managerial experience you possess. No matter how timely your idea proves to be according to market dictates, your business may hit a brick wall if you are not prepared personally. So, beyond market timing and customer readiness, you must consider your own timing.

CHAPTER SEVEN

ADVICE – THE BEST PEOPLE TO TAKE IT FROM

The business world is akin to a jungle where only the fittest survive. The present unpleasant global economic outlook has even made things more difficult. For young, inexperienced entrepreneurs and experienced professionals who are new to the business of entrepreneurship, keeping a lean budget and being super smart is not a choice but a necessity. A young entrepreneur is expected to wear many hats; accountant, dispatch rider, marketing executive, communication strategist, HR manager and many more. It is not unusual for entrepreneurs to sometimes feel overwhelmed or pressured when they need answers to many nagging business questions. Every entrepreneur, therefore, needs to have a network of experienced individuals who they can turn to when in a fix.

You will be able to scale faster and leapfrog some of the expected challenges of business if you engage people who have better experience and qualifications in industry than yourself. You can learn from their failures and successes to make better decisions as you forge ahead in your journey. Sometimes, individuals who look into your business with an unprejudiced mind that important things which you have repeatedly overlooked.

Besides, in my experience working with and mentoring young entrepreneurs, one recurrent trend I have noticed is that most young entrepreneurs lack confidence and are not well grounded enough to navigate the grey areas of business. Many great ideas have withered in the minds of young entrepreneurs because they had no one to give them heads up on how to fine-tune the approach and guide them to nurture those ideas to maturity. If you have someone or a group of people who give you actionable and honest advice from time to time, you will save a lot of time, money and energy in the short and long haul. Regular spurts of guidance and motivation will help young entrepreneurs and those who are new to the world of self-employment reach their full potential much faster.

Below, I note some of those who may be in the best position to give sound advice as you navigate the narrow and oft-challenging crevices of entrepreneurship.

Mentor (s): Having a mentor (or mentors) is one of the surest shortcuts to business success. Mentors can fast-track your success as they can open doors of endless opportunities for you, teach you valuable skills and give you honest feedback and sound advice on your ideas and strategies. I have said a lot about mentorship in Chapter 5 already and will not spend much time rehashing all I have stated earlier.

You won't find a mentor by mere wishful thinking, so brace up and speak up. Look within your network, reach out to business leaders that you admire and ask for help to reach them if you have to. However, while paying for just any mentoring is not an ideal, try not to tune out if your proposed mentor seeks payment. If you are convinced that the person has the experience in your line of business, and is honest without bias, I believe that a great tutor is worth the compensation.

Colleagues: Avivit Ben-Aharon, the Clinical Director of Gr8 Speech Incorporated once said that connecting and sharing ideas with his colleagues has been a great source of strength for him; "I have found speaking and connecting with like-minded professionals and learning from them to be the best source of information." It is not unusual to find spectacular business advice and direction from individuals who are on the same journey as you; individuals with who you share similar values, face similar challenges, have the same thought process and pursue similar goals. I'm quite sure you will find mastermind groups that you can join either online or offline where you can leverage on the strengths, skills and experiences of others to achieve growth.

Accomplished Entrepreneurs in the same industry: Also, approaching high flying and successful entrepreneurs who operate in the same field as you can also be another smart move to make when seeking advice. They have been in business for ages and have processes and systems that are similar to yours. They most likely have - in times past - faced the kind of obstacles you are facing. So instead of toughing it and walking it alone, it might benefit you greatly to seek counsel from them.

To be candid, many of those you approach in this capacity may be unwilling to share their success secrets with you because you both compete in the same market. It is, therefore, better to be on the lookout for entrepreneurs who operate in regions that are not very close to yours; this, however, does not mean you won't find a business owner who is willing to help you in your region. What I am only trying to state is that it may be a bit difficult.

Business publications: Business publications explicitly made for start-ups (magazines, journals, podcasts) are also a good repository of knowledge. Such publications cover a wide range of business topics, and in them, you can find resources that answer to your questions. Furthermore, you get to learn from professionals who are the cream of the crop in their niches; each one of them with different views and experiences that you can learn from to achieve higher levels of success.

Take publications like Success Magazine, Entrepreneur Magazine, Forbes Magazine, Harvard Business Review for example. These publications address matters that are relevant, timely, and helpful to small business owners. They also interview individuals who have built successful businesses thereby giving young business owners deep insights on what it takes to build successful enterprises while also serving as sources of inspiration and motivation from where small business owners can draw strength. These magazines also give advice on some of the most significant issues in the lives of entrepreneurs; how to handle stress, how to avoid burnout, healthy diet tips, etc.

Apart from the publications that I mentioned above, there are a ton of many others out there in hard and soft copies. For those who do not have enough time to read, many of these resources are available in audio formats that you can listen to while you work-out or during a commute. Just pick the ones you find helpful and subscribe for the hard, soft or audio copies. Most importantly, don't just read these things for the sake of reading, make it a point to apply the things you have learned consciously, remember that knowledge is no longer power, instead, it is the application of knowledge that confers power and success.

Experts/Professionals: I correctly understand that you need to operate on a lean budget as a start-up, but there are some specific things that you should not compromise so you don't end up being penny wise and pound foolish in the long run. Depending on the severity and importance of what you are up against and your level of expertise about it, there will be times when it is better for you to seek the expertise or counsel of experts. For example, if you are not a lawyer or an accountant yourself, it would be wise for you not to tackle legal or tax issues without the advice of an expert. Because asides the fact that you might end up wasting a lot of money, you might eventually end up in jail if you make the slightest, albeit honest mistake. Ignorance of the law is not an excuse you know.

Furthermore, if you deal with plants and machinery in your line of business, do not cut corners or compromise quality when technical issues arise. If you engage quack technicians in handling production equipment and they end up ruining it, production may be delayed for a long while, you may go bankrupt, and in extreme cases, it may spell the total collapse of your business. To avoid unpleasant situations, always seek the guidance and opinion of experts on the best steps to take especially on issues that are way beyond your control and or out of your scope. This also applies to managerial concerns like employee-management. Whenever you need to, go to expert professionals who can help you find solutions that perfectly fit your needs. The road to business success is already riddled with enough potholes, so don't make things worse for yourself by taking on avoidable snags.

Customers: I once saw a quote on the wall in an office. The quote says, "On our premises, the customer is the most important visitor - we are dependent on him, he is not dependent on us." What this reiterates emphatically is the age-old maxim, "the customer is King". Interestingly, the maxim has evolved in Japan to become "Customer is God".

You will have no business if there are no customers for you to serve in the first place. Customer satisfaction should be an ideal that you always strive towards. But before we go further, I would like to ask, how would you satisfy customers if you do not listen to them and put their advice to use in your business? Examples abound of companies that have folded up because they failed to listen to their customers or sought customer advice but refused, whether by omission or commission, to actualise those pieces of advice.

If you have some time to spare, kindly check out Dan Berger, the founder of SocialTables online. Fresh out of Georgetown's McDonough School of Business with an MBA in the bag, Dan wanted to do nothing else but plan events. He had a vision of changing the face of events planning by proposing a system that will allow event attendees choose their sitting arrangement. Not minding how appealing the idea looked at the moment, Dan had no choice than to discard this forward-thinking approach when his customers advised him not to press on with the idea. Having planned more than one million events so far, Dan's company has become a leader in the events planning niche of the hospitality industry. Not long ago, the venture raised over $13 million in funding - to tell you how profitable the firm has become. Long and short, even if you do not seek advice from any other person or group of persons, do not with your own hands send your enterprise to an early grave by failing to seek the counsel of your customers. Make your customers feel important, treat them with respect, put their advice to work and watch your business soar.

Employees: If you want to win in the marketplace, then you must win first in the workplace. As one of the most critical stakeholders in your business, your employees have solid knowledge about the business and may even have a better understanding of how the company works than you. This should not come as a surprise because employees are the ones that interface with customers and feel their pulse and yearnings on a daily basis.

Note that employees sometimes may not be bold enough to approach you out of the blues to give you advice (this depends on your leadership approach though), it then falls on you to continuously relate with them and ask what they think and how they believe the company can move. Make this a habit and you would be surprised at how much your employees can help the business grow. Every employee wants to be appreciated, and one of the best ways to show that you value them is to let them have a "say" in the business. To corroborate my point, I would restate the thought of Simon Sinek who said, "When people are emotionally invested, they want to contribute". Hire great employees, trust them and listen to them more often.

Investors: Being who they are and given the position they hold in your business, your investors will give feedback whether you ask or not and it is exceedingly important that you listen. Investors by what they do (investing in companies) have over the years garnered business expertise within and probably, beyond your industry and can recognise business pointers that you may not see which places them in a better position to show you the way. Before you shun their guidance and direction as unsolicited prying, remember that they have staked their hard-earned money on your enterprise and hence are most unlikely to give you advice that will plunge the company in troubled waters.

Let me give you a personal example. There is a friend of mine who is an engineer. He loves to write as well and is a damn good writer to the extent that he left his plump job in a leading construction firm to start his online book publishing outfit. Sales were not so great until he met this particular investor who staked some money into the business and also offered my friend some valuable advice. On taking the investor's opinion, his customer traction picked up sporadically, and he can now afford to pay himself a bit more than he earned in his previous job.

Even at times when you are sure beyond doubt that the view you hold is superior to theirs, you to need to drive forward your stance with caution and let them know that you have listened to their thoughts and understand their concerns. The importance of maintaining a cordial relationship with your investors cannot be overemphasized.

It is often said that the best leaders are necessarily not those who talk the best or have all the answers but those who are smart enough to listen to wise counsel and are not too proud to ask when they need help. So, to be the best entrepreneur that you have the potential capacity to be, part of your fulltime job must be to seek and listen to advise from different constituents like employees, experts, colleagues, mentors, and investors. The role of leading a company is usually severe but with a cult of advisors around you, the burden will be much lessened.

As a final point, I would implore you always to take some time to reflect and think through the advice and suggestions that you receive. Sometimes, the opinion of others might conflict with yours; it is normal. In times like that, listen more to your gut after weighing all the pros and cons. It may be your gut (or what some people call sixth sense) that will give you the best answers. Above all, learn to be in tune with your inner self as much as you seek advice.

CHAPTER EIGHT

YOUR WEBSITE AS A DIGITAL STOREFRONT

Without trivialising how challenging it is, you will agree with me that starting a new business venture from scratch is fun and intriguing. Not many things can compare with the magic of watching your abstract idea develop into something concrete. However, once the business idea has been concretised and launched, the next most challenging hurdle is getting the world to know your business.

For your digital and traditional marketing efforts to materialise into real leads and sales, you need to build a website for your business. Your site is like a digital office where you get to show potential customers and clients what you have to offer. Unlike a physical store where people walk in and out, people stumble upon your website as they surf the net.

In this age that we live in, a sizable percentage of sales revenue is derived from online transactions. In fact, a majority of offline transactions are a result of marketing efforts made online. Over 2.4 billion people use the internet on a daily basis and out of those, 2.18 billion have searched online to buy something, and 0.96 billion purchased goods over the internet last month. For the records, more than 1.78 billion people will search you online before doing business with you. Moreover, the world of business is set to experience a massive digital turnaround as the fourth industrial revolution races towards us.

Notwithstanding the size of your business and no matter what product or service you offer, it is imperative that you have a website. From the mundane to the important and the outrageously luxurious, there is absolutely nothing that you cannot sell online. If you don't have a website, I bet you will lose a lot of patronage to your competitors who have one – that is if you are not losing sales to them already.

Even if you operate in an industry where you think online presence does not have much impact on sales, you should still have a website so that your business, vision, mission and product or service offerings can be visible to potential customers, partners, employees and even investors.

When it comes to competing with bigger businesses, the internet has given small and medium enterprises a level playing field. With a professional website, your little business can wear the feel and project the image of a much bigger firm.

You think you do not need a website because you don't sell online? Have a rethink, please! So many people don't buy online as well but search for information online before purchasing in physical stores. So, your website might be the first chance you have to make an excellent first impression.

Let me also state here categorically that it is not enough to have a website. If your site looks like a two-year old's fine art project, your opportunity to make a lasting first impression may be forever lost. For your business to look professional and be taken as credible, your website has to be well designed, mobile friendly, simple, and easy to navigate. Trust me, it is better for you not to have a site at all than to have a shabby one. A well-designed website tells the customer, "We care so much about you and take what we do so seriously. Welcome to our digital home!". A poorly designed website on the other hand screams, "We don't even know why we are here. Welcome yourself!"

IMPORTANCE OF A WEBSITE

Now let's explore further to see how a website can give your business(es) an edge in the digital age that we live in.

Marketing

Marketing is the most important reason for having a website. Or what is the essence of having a site if it doesn't translate to business leads and more patronage? A business website markets your products and promotes visibility. The internet's global reach can as well extend the reach and impact of your business to places and areas that you might otherwise not be able to access physically.

Therefore, promote your website as much as possible. Let your web address/URL be on all your brand materials, add it in your email signature and encourage your employees to do same.

Accessibility

As you build your new business, you will have to work round the clock to drive sales and increase revenue. However, the good news is that having a website can reduce your task and grind by almost half because a site is to a considerable extent permanent, has no opening or closing time and as such can be visited at anytime from anywhere across the globe. You won't need to go from house to house with your products in a bag for marketing; all you need do is to update the website with your latest products and refer people to your site. It also makes it easy for you to track certain aspects of your business without much effort and with minimal to no extra cost.

Relationships

With a website, you are better positioned to meet your customers' needs faster and more efficiently to forge stronger ties. If you have a site, your clients and customers can reach you at any time of the day from wherever and it makes it easier for them to provide you with instant feedback.

The opportunity for seamless and efficient interaction that a website provides will help you bond with customers better, and they will trust your business the more.

Performance Measurement

By embedding tools like Google analytics or Jetpack to your website, you are able to collect valuable information on how visitors relate with your business. The number of visitors to your site, how much time they spent on your site, the pages they clicked, and more are factors that can help you monitor and evaluate business performance.

A business website can give you insights into what visitors feel about your products - information that can be very helpful when you are working on content strategy, products improvement or marketing and sales campaign.

Competitive Edge

If with all that has been said, you are still not convinced as to why your business needs a website, know for sure that your competitors are most definitely on the internet. If your competitors are online and you are not, know for sure that you are losing a considerable share of the market to them. One of the best ways to be at par with the competition and even stay ahead of them is to host a well-designed, interactive and search engine optimized website where you can woe customers and grab a substantial share of the market.

Portfolio

Given the limitations of space and time, it can sometimes be difficult to showcase your products and expertise to a wide audience. A website can then be an online portfolio where you have the opportunity to flaunt your products with a flick of your fingers anywhere you find yourself.

Authenticity and Professionalism

As stated previously, many consumers now make it a point to size up companies on the internet before deciding to patronise. Do you know why? It's quite straightforward; they want to be sure that the business is genuine. Also, it is not unusual for prospective investors to check your online presence before committing their funds to your business. Dedicating a website to your business goes a long way to legitimise the firm while giving your brand an aura of professionalism.

In continuance, the process of establishing your online presence does not end with creating a website for your business. Profiting from your online presence takes time and continuous effort like incorporating the appropriate search engine optimisation (SEO) tactics. You must consider the design as well; how appealing to the eyes is it?

To tell you the truth, there are times I have refused to deal with businesses because their website looks tacky.

Your company's website can either make or break the business as it says a lot about those running the business. Trust me, things like website are what your audience judge your business against. So, designing a website with an appealing user interface can yield better conversion rates and lead to higher patronage and more robust revenue.

As I set to start writing this part, I remembered a discussion I once had with my friend Sam, a while ago. We both were talking about web design and in the course of our conversation, to emphasise how important a well-designed website is to a business, he told me that there is one particular website he visits every day, whether he needs to transact with the company or not. In his exact words "I find the beauty of that website captivating and even, almost therapeutic." That precisely is what people should say about your website.

If you must yield maximum returns from your online presence, then you should know that it will require investment regarding money, time and energy. Good things often come at a dear cost. But trust me, it is worth all the hard work. For your hard-work to pay off, you need to seek the service of an efficient website designer (N.B: if you are not a web designer, do not design your website yourself. Remember what we discussed in the previous chapter about letting expert professionals handle essential things?

ASPECTS YOUR WEBSITE HELPS WITH

Your site is one of those fundamental things) to help you manage the most critical aspects of your website which are discussed as follows:

Content and Visual Elements

Content and visual elements have to do with pictures, fonts and other details that are by nature, typographic i.e. features that relate to words, pictures and their appearance. These aspects are important because they influence how the message on your website is delivered to your audience and how your audience interpret the message. As we now live in a visual age, your audience will most likely not remember long, winding and prosaic content. Today's digital natives relate more with material that is concise, pictorial and relatable, though, all these have to be done in moderation; the right amount of words and the right mix of pictures is what counts. Fewer words and too many pictures or too many words and fewer pictures can make your webpage look gaudy and challenging to read. Good website designers know all these things and can work magic with them. If you are therefore not a web designer, let one handle the design of your website.

Navigation

The next most important aspect of your website is the navigation. How easy is it for those who visit your site to find information they require? Talking about webpage navigation is akin to talking about how you arrange things in a house. How would you feel if you enter a home and see clothes in the fridge, find a blender in the restroom or see a septic tank dug right in the middle of the kitchen? What you will feel is what visitors think when they visit a website that has a poorly developed navigation.

Your webpage should be quite easy to navigate; well labelled, fun to explore and easy to understand. Brilliant yet straightforward navigation will surely make visitors always come back to your website.

Brand Uniformity

When Lisa Gansky said, "A brand is a voice, and a product is a souvenir", what she means is that your brand is what projects your business; how people see and perceive your business. It is what pops up in people's head when they hear your business name or see your logo. It is what sets you apart from your competitors and is usually identified through your logo. As we talk about logos, visualise the Apple or Microsoft logo. If you see those logos without the name of their respective companies inscribed anywhere around them, you can still tell the companies they belong to and that precisely is what you as a young entrepreneur should aspire to achieve.

It is quite essential that your audience can tell you apart (with your logo and unique colour) from any other business in your industry. So, while you design your website, make sure that all the elements of your logo are integrated into the site. Besides, it is equally important that you be consistent in your brand and visual communication. Do not use a different logo and colour on your website then change your style on other materials. Be consistent! It is quite important.

Engagement

It is requisite that website design and development be approached carefully by every business. The pages on your website must be laid out superbly in such a way that your audience will want to engage with the site. How engaging visitors find your website inevitably determines to a large extent, whether they will be converted or not.

Organization and Search Engine Optimization

A competent website designer knows that the way a website is organised increases the chances of information dissemination to customers. So, a talented website designer will put valuable information where they are easy to find. For instance, because most of us are programmed to start reading from left to right (speakers and readers of Arabic can be an exception because they read and write from right to left), putting the essential information on a webpage in the top left area can improve the chances of visitors reading it.

Apart from organising the website layout correctly, essential details must be placed in visible areas on the website. You can make this happen by embedding the keywords that relate to your business in the HTML (Hyper Text Markup Language). With excellent search engine optimisation, search engines like Google, Yahoo, Bing can easily crawl into your website and rank it higher, thereby making your site more visible and easily searchable online.

As you, therefore, set to build and grow your business to success, one of the most important things that you must do is to host a website for the company. As more people are joining the internet community every day, having a site for your start-up is undoubtedly a smart business investment that will give you equal opportunities to compete against the most prominent brands.

CHAPTER NINE

MASTERMINDING AND NETWORKING - THE HALLMARKS OF BUSINESS SUCCESS

Sometimes in 1908, Napoleon Hill got the chance to interview Andrew Carnegie a famous business magnate and philanthropist and inquire how he grew to become one of the most powerful men in the world at that time. It was at this meeting that Andrew Carnegie inspired Hill to survey more than 500 millionaires who were considered some of the most successful business owners across the globe at that time. After about 20 years of toiling laboriously on this project, Hill came up with several documents that outlined some of the patterns of process and experience that are peculiar to the over 500 successful entrepreneurs he surveyed. It was this project that culminated in Napoleon Hill's most popular book "Think and Grow Rich" which has become a sort of religious text for entrepreneurs across the globe.

While many people think that the first formal mention of the term, mastermind is found in Napoleon Hill's "Think and Grow Rich," that appears not to be the case. In 1927, about ten years before he published Think and Grow Rich, Hill had first touched briefly on the subject of Master Mind in his book, "The Laws of Success". In "The Laws of Success", Hill says the Master Mind "is a friendly alliance among people to support each other with their plans". He states further that the group "helps to organize useful knowledge, creating a virtual encyclopedia from which each member can draw information."

Moreover, in 1930, exactly seven years before "Think and Grow Rich" was published, Hill talked about the Master Mind again in another of his books titled, "The Magic Ladder of Success". In that publication Hill says that, "the process of mind blending here described as a Master Mind may be likened to the act of a single transmission wire, thereby stepping up the power passing over that line by the amount of energy the batteries carry ... Each mind, through the principle of mind chemistry, stimulates all the other minds in the group."

I think the reason most people believe that Hill's first mention of the mastermind principle is found in "Think and Grow Rich" which was published in 1937 is that "Think and Grow Rich" happens to be Hill's most popular and most successful publication. Again, the amount of information he provides in the book about mastermind principle is much more than he provided in his previous books. It is in "Think and Grow Rich" that he explores the subject thoroughly. Napoleon says in "Think and Grow Rich" that; "The mastermind principle consists of an alliance of two or more minds working in perfect harmony for the attainment of a common definite objective. No two minds ever come together without a third invisible force which may be likened to a 'third mind'. When a group of individual minds are coordinated, and function in harmony, the increased energy created through that alliance becomes available to every individual in the group."

To further give credence to the efficacy of the mastermind principle, Napoleon Hill said of Henry Ford; "Through his association with Edison, Burbank, Burroughs, and Firestone, Mr. Ford added to his brain power the sum and substance of the intelligence, experience, knowledge, and spiritual forces of these four men. Moreover, he appropriated and made use of the Master Mind principle."

Above and beyond, Andrew Carnegie, who commissioned Napoleon Hill to undertake the interview project mentioned above was also a firm believer of the mastermind principle and attributes a great deal of his success in business to it. Carnegie went as far as constituting a 50-man group saddled with the sole responsibility of developing ideas that will grow his steel business. To say that Napoleon Hill got wind of the plan from his interaction with Andrew Carnegie would not be far from the truth.

While the appellation "mastermind alliance" may be attributed solely to Napoleon Hill, the concept is however believed to have an older history. The concept dates far back to the ancient Greeks and the reign of British ruler, King Arthur. During his reign, King Arthur formed a group called "Knights of the Round Table"; a group of individuals with whom the King brainstormed and formulated ideas and policies to move the British empire forward.

The fact that the mastermind principle is still relevant today as it was when introduced over a century ago shows that the proclamations of the law are valid and effective. The principle has been applied across all strata of human endeavor especially business and politics. Across the world today, hardly will you find a President, Prime Minister or King who does not have a group of non-political advisors who consult for the country especially on issues of the economy.

When Roger Hamilton was working in Silicon Valley, he met a big-time investor who set up a $100 million venture capital firm. He asked the man what his biggest challenge was, and the man said: "my biggest challenge is finding investable entrepreneurs." One of the ways to become on par with Silicon Valley entrepreneurs is to take advantage of masterminding.

Popular Singapore based author, speaker and social entrepreneur, Roger Hamilton, often referred to as "Asia's leading wealth consultant" in one of his video series stated the reason he started an entrepreneur mastermind group. According to him, the epiphany came in Silicon Valley while he was discussing with an investor who runs a $100 million venture capital firm. In the course of their discussion, Hamilton said he asked what the man's biggest challenge in business was and to which the man replied, "finding investable entrepreneurs." He said the investor stated that many young entrepreneurs have little to no knowledge of some of the necessary skills and principles that guarantee success.

Few years after this chance discussion with the venture capitalist, Hamilton formed a mastermind group where young entrepreneurs get to meet with some of the most successful entrepreneurs in the world and other budding entrepreneurs like themselves to learn new skills, share experiences and network.

As a young entrepreneur, you should know that being a business owner goes beyond managing books, keeping records and giving direction. You are mostly the backbone of the business, and more often than not, your employees look up to you for inspiration, motivation, ideation and knowledge; and trust me, all these expectations of you that people have can sometimes make you feel pressured. Master Mind groups can, however, be your saving grace and sounding board where you can share the weight of your challenges with your peers, sharpen your skills and stay abreast of the latest trends in business that you can exploit to move your firm forward.

Through mastermind groups, people have achieved the level of personal and business success they aspire to by brainstorming with other like-minded individuals, setting goals, encouraging a positive attitude towards life, supporting each other in trying times and holding each other accountable. Essentially, the raison d'etre of mastermind groups is for members to help each other grow and succeed in all endeavors and ramifications of life.

Unlike what obtains in networking or mentoring settings, members of mastermind groups are equals. While it is characteristic of them sometimes to invite more experienced business owners to give them advice, mastermind group members usually come together at defined intervals to lend support to one another, solicit and receive critique on new business ideas and remain accountable to one another. For example, the Young Presidents Organization (YPO), one of the most prominent mastermind groups in the world is an association of CEOs of companies with annual sales turnover not less than $8, 000, 000 and a workforce of at least 50 employees. Members of the YPO leverage the strengths and complement the weaknesses of one another to achieve growth in business. World leaders like late Fidel Castro, King Abdullah II of Jordan, President George Bush and Nelson Mandela are some of the world leaders that members of the YPO have learnt and received treasured insights from about business and personal life.

Other examples of prominent mastermind groups in history that shaped the success of their members are The Vagabonds and The Inklings.

The Vagabonds: The Vagabonds, formed in 1915, was a mastermind group of five business leaders - President Warren Harding, Henry Ford, Luther Burbank, Thomas Edison and Harvey Firestone – who met regularly to discuss business and politics and also engage in recreational activities. The group was however dissolved in 1924 owing to the death of

President Warren Harding and the overwhelming media attention the group had started to receive.

The Inklings: The Inklings was another famous mastermind group of literary giants in England who often met to read, to offer criticism and comments and generally discuss on how to take their writings to much greater heights. Members of the group were Charles Williams, Owen Barfield, CS Lewis and JRR Tolkien. History books have it that members of the group were instrumental to the success of JRR Tolkien's "The Lord of the Rings" and "The Chronicles of Narnia" by CS Lewis.

If the likes of Henry Ford, Harvey Firestone, CS Lewis, President Warren Harding and Thomas Edison did not downplay the importance of masterminding to success, who are you not to join or create one?

BENEFITS OF A MASTERMIND GROUP

You are an entrepreneur and yet to join any mastermind group? Below are some of the enormous opportunities you have been missing out on. If you are a member of one, however, you can use the list to judge the effectiveness of your group.

Goal Setting

The life of an entrepreneur is a fast one fraught with many surprises and uncertainties. You wake up each morning not knowing what the day may bring. In that high energy, rollercoaster kind of life, you are bound to miss some crucial goals and milestones if you do not have someone or a group of people who can hold you to account and remind you of such goals from time to time. Most mastermind groups are built around breaking down big goals to small manageable steps that must be taken weekly. Members forge ahead together by setting individual goals and holding one another accountable to ensure that those goals are met in due time. Membership of a mastermind group can, therefore, help you dominate and reach your goals faster. Moreover, if you encounter any difficulty in your quest to achieve your own set goals, you have a horde of loyal peers who will go the extra mile to help you overcome your challenges and ensure that you reach your set goals. In another vein, you will most likely do what needs to be done, no matter how difficult or inconvenient it seems, towards achieving your goals when you remember that you are accountable to a group of people who will not take things lightly with you if you fail to play your part well.

Grow your Magic

It is an enduring truth that relationships are pivotal to business success. As an entrepreneur, you need to continually meet with new people and forge strategic alliances with them and masterminding is one of the easiest ways to exponentially grow your network. Whether your group is an exclusive one with six members or an open one with fifty members does not really matter because once you become a member of the group, the connections of other group members indirectly become your connections too and before you know it, your reputation will travel far and wide and business will take a surge.

Referrals

Each person in a mastermind group works in a separate industry and has a peculiar set of skill. For instance, Duke is a furniture maker while you run a media consultancy. If you have just leased a new business space and you need new items of furniture, who will you patronize? Duke of course! Likewise, if Duke has just rolled out some new furniture collections and wants to do a catalogue or seeks advertisement, he is sure to confer with you. It does not end there because as you and Duke belong to the same group his customers and entire network have become your potential customers and vice versa.

Support Base

Once you decide to become an entrepreneur, family members, friends and associates start to think you've gone crazy. They bombard you with a barrage of what if(s), how(s) and why(s) and ask questions like; "Why do you want to leave such a good job to go start something that may not work?" "What if you fail?" "How will you survive?" "Are you sure you have what it takes?" "Remember you have a family to support", etc. Once you decide to take this journey, a team of doubters will grow behind you who can sometimes dissolve your confidence and make you want to throw in the proverbial towel.

The pressure mounts harder if business starts and does not pick up the pace as fast as you projected. At this point, doubters will question your sanity and ask how long you will remain "unreasonable". Blame them not, for it is like human beings to cast doubts and speak ill of what they cannot comprehend. Those who do not understand your journey and what drives you will most likely misjudge your intents and actions.

Besides the issue of doubters, the freedom that comes with being an entrepreneur sometimes breeds isolation and worries. Worries about not knowing when or where your next paycheck will come from. Peculiar business challenges that you may not be able to discuss with your employees, friends and even family members. As a member of a mastermind group, however, you will meet and mix with people with whom you share similar struggles. People who understand that being an entrepreneur is the only way to real freedom and high achievements. Individuals in this group would be your motivation when you are low and your cheerleaders when you win. The support base that a mastermind group represents reminds me of an African proverb which says, "A dog that receives assistance can kill a gorilla."

Mentorship Opportunity

I have talked extensively on the importance of mentorship to your success as an entrepreneur in previous chapters. And without equivocation, mastermind groups can be the perfect place to meet mentor(s). Like it or not, in the mastermind group that you belong, you would meet individuals who perform at a higher level and those who are on a lower pedestal than yourself which presents a rare opportunity for you to help and get help; to mentor and be mentored.

Brainstorming

As people with diverse experience and skill set, members of the same mastermind group can quickly tap into one another's experience to generate new business ideas, draw knowledge and gain innovation on how to increase productivity and business outcomes. When you grind your sharp mind against that of other members, it should be expected that a volcanic eruption of creative ingenuity will occur that will empower each member to achieve their personal and business goals.

CONSIDERATIONS BEFORE JOINING A MASTERMIND GROUP

Moving forward, I will like to state here that there are certain things you must put into perspective before you join or start a mastermind group. Failure to consider these things may inhibit you from achieving the outlandish goals you aspire to.

Have a Destination

We all know the story of Alice and the Cat in "Alice in Wonderland";

> *"Would you tell me, please, which way I ought to go*
> *from here?"*
> *"That depends a good deal on where you want to get to."*
> *"I don't much care where."*
> *"Then it doesn't matter which way you go." Said the cat*
> *'So long as I get SOMEWHERE,'*
> *Alice added as an explanation.*
> *'Oh, you're sure to do that,' said the cat,*
> *'If you only walk long enough.'*

After evaluating where you are, the next thing is to decide where you want to be. How do you envision your business to be five years from now? What milestones do you seek to achieve in the coming year? And what heights do you aspire to? Create your vision and chart the direction that will take you there. People who achieve success in business and life are those who are clear on what they want from life.

Where Do You Stand

You wake up in the morning and need to get to Massachusetts. You dash into your car and click open the GPS map, but there's a challenge; you know your destination is Massachusetts, but you do not know your starting point. As much as it is vital that you know where you are going, I dare say it is more important that you know where you are. It is by knowing where you are that you will know how to reach your destination.

Be honest with yourself and do not play the denial game. Let your present condition make you angry; let it fuel your drive and move you to action. You know where you are headed, so the only thing left is to see where you stand; that is how to see the route that will take you from where you are to where you wish to be.

Create a Plan of Action

Now that you are clear on where you are and where you want to reach, the next step is to find the best route to achieve your desired goals. Plotting your course will save you from wandering and help you avoid distractions that may slow you down on the road to success.

Create a detailed plan of how you will get to your desired location and outline the things and names of the people that will help you on that journey.

Know Your Why

Why are you an entrepreneur? Why do you want to build a billion-dollar enterprise? I ask you these two essential questions because it is difficult to keep your momentum if you do not know why you are in business in the first instance. Do I need to remind you that entrepreneurship is not a walk in the park? There are days when you would feel like dumping it all. Days when you will feel the urge to run away; far from your creditors, employees and customers. On difficult and trying days, it is your why that keeps you going and makes the journey worthwhile. Without a why trust me, you may not last in the business of doing business.

Now that you know where you stand, have a vision of where you are going, have plotted a plan on how to get there and understand why you want to get there before joining a mastermind alliance, you are poised to get the best out of masterminding.

Choosing the Right Group

Nowadays, mastermind groups are a dime a dozen. They are scattered in all small towns and big cities across the globe, each claiming to have what you need. However, not all these groups are as active as they profess. You know, some people wake up and bored to the bones and created a mastermind group to feed their egos, while away time and kill boredom. It is therefore vital that you know what to look out for before joining a mastermind group that fits your growth needs.

First of all, do not join a group where you will be the smartest person; if you do, you will do yourself a lot of disservices. Members of the same mastermind group are supposed to be almost on the same pedestal if not on the same. The essence of masterminds is for members to grow together by helping each other grow; it is different from mentorship where one person is expected to help other(s) develop. However, if you don't have the financial muscle to join the big-league mastermind groups like Young Presidents Organization (YPO), you can look around you for other brilliant entrepreneurs and form one.

People

Again, permit me to reiterate that you shouldn't join a group where you will be the smartest person. To move ahead, you need to be in a group that has a mix of people who are on the same level as you and those who are more successful than you are. Being around people whose level you aspire to, who you can learn from and respect is how you would escape complacency as such people will inspire and shove you to ensure you reach your goals.

Time and format

To get the best out of a mastermind group, choose one that fits well into your schedule. It doesn't make much sense if you register in a group and end up missing meetings and other important gatherings because your plan often clashes with group meetings. If you have more time during weekends, don't join a group that meets during the week and if your weekends are clumsier than weekdays, it is better you join a group that meets during the week.

Moreover, you have to consider the format that works best for you. Some masterminds connect through video or teleconferencing and WhatsApp group chats, some prefer to meet in person while others relate with a mix of online and offline methods. Know what works best for you and go for it.

Non-Disclosure Agreement

One of the most important (if not the most important) checks to make before joining a group is to find out if the group has a non-disclosure agreement. In mastermind groups, you and other members will exchange vital information and ideas that may be compromised if people outside the group know those things. Therefore, I highly recommend that you join a group that has a non-disclosure agreement where you are sure that the information and ideas you share are safe.

***

Mastermind groups come in different forms. While some are strictly exclusive like the Young Presidents Organization (YPO), we have others that are open. Some are entirely free to join, some only require that you pay a registration fee and to enter some, you have to pay a registration fee and are expected to pay a whopping annual subscription fee. If you cannot find what you require in free groups, then by all means, consider a paid one and see the financial obligation as a core investment in your business since being a member will open a vista of new business opportunities for you.

In another vein, you can even consider forming a group if you believe you have enough drive, the required knowledge and money to do so.

Founders of mastermind groups are often influential business leaders and their responsibility in the group is to set a tone for the group and have the responsibility to guide those who are involved to overcome their individual business and personal challenges and connect them with individuals who possess the knowledge that will help them reach their goals faster and better.

If you are sure you up to the task of starting and running the affairs of a mastermind group, then get to work. Fire up your computer and make a rough sketch of how many members you will allow. Will, the group, be exclusive or open; free or paid? Who are the people you will invite to join your group? What are the attributes you will look out for in those prospective members? Where and how will you meet? What are the rules and regulations that will guide the conduct of members? And most importantly, what will be the purpose of the group?

To uphold high standards for your group, to maintain trust and ensure effectiveness, endeavor to treat the group as a professional entity. Set reasonable expectations for all members upfront and make it very clear that members are expected to help each other. The beauty of a mastermind group is not for some members to get what they want while others do not. The real beauty radiates when all members share the camaraderie to give as much as they receive towards helping each other succeed. It is by so doing that the group will live up to the fundamental principles of masterminding as put succinctly by Stephen Covey:

"This is the habit of creative cooperation or team-work. Synergy results from valuing differences by bringing different perspectives together in the spirit of mutual respect."

THE MAGIC OF CONTINUOUS LEARNING

Now you have become your boss. Business is running smoothly and is yielding substantial profits; enough for you to afford some of the niceties of life. You have mastered the business process like the back of your hand and can sleep at night without any worries. However, it is at this point that complacency, the biggest enemy of progress, sets in.

How then do you avoid complacency? A staunch commitment to continuous learning is the only answer. The most critical element of success that marks average entrepreneurs from great ones is that great entrepreneurs never stop learning.

In his address to the 366th graduating class at Harvard University in 2017, Mark Zuckerberg said that "And as technology keeps changing, we need to focus more on continuous education throughout our lives." Zuck, as he is called by friends and colleagues signs up for courses till today.

Warren Buffet, one of the wealthiest men in the world today estimates that he spends an average of six hours every day reading. Once he met with a group of students and in the course of discussion pointed to a stack of books and reports and told the students to "Read 500 pages like this, every day. That's how knowledge works. It builds up, like compound interest. All of you can do it, but I guarantee not many of you will do it."

Remember that when you were still an employee, your company periodically sends you on training, workshops and seminars. Those training and seminars are even more important that you are the owner of a business. As a business owner, the challenges you will face are more complex, and all your employees will look up to you for direction and guidance. You, therefore, need to be on your toes at all time by adding new skills, knowledge and expertise to your repertoire. The strength of a business lies in the power of the people running it. In today's ever-changing world where markets have become extremely dynamic, it has become exigent to stay current and abreast of the latest developments to keep up with the pace at which business moves.

Nevertheless, continuous learning necessarily does not have to be a certificate course, an online course, seminar or workshop. It includes reading and learning new things on a daily basis. Engaging in regular self-reflection is a form of continuous learning.

Again, make a conscious commitment to continue learning; to read something new every day and be better informed than you were yesterday. Mark Zuckerberg, Warren Buffet, Jeff Bezos, Richard Branson, Mary Kay Ash, Robert Kiyosaki, Bill Gates all ascribe part of their success to their ability to continue learning. To join the ranks of these successful business leaders, make learning a part of your daily routine.

IDENTIFYING YOUR STRENGTHS AND WEAKNESSES

Boldly engraved at the entrance of the court to the sacred temple of Apollo in Delphi is the maxim "Know Thyself". As an entrepreneur, being aware of your strengths and weaknesses is of essential importance. It is an exercise that will help you understand where you can be most effective and recognize the areas of your business where you need help.

To set this topic in motion, let me share the story of two tech giants – Bill Gates and Steve Jobs. Both of them have built business empires, made a fortune, impacted the entire world and are similarly known for producing radical computing innovations within the same period. However, will it interest you to know that while both have made almost identical marks, they have different entrepreneurial skills and strengths. While Bill is known to have been an avid coder, spending an average of 8 hours daily writing code since he was a teenager, Steve on the other hand never wrote a line of code his entire life but had an unusual knack for product design and design thinking. Imagine what the world would have missed if both of these gurus failed to discover their strengths and limitations. Would there have been a Microsoft if Gates did not focus on coding and Jobs struggled to be a programmer? Maybe or maybe not.

I will also like to use Mark Zuckerberg as another example. In 2008, Mark featured on the program 60 Minutes anchored by Leslie Stahl and in the voice-over of the interview, Leslie says: "We were warned that he can be awkward and reluctant to talk about himself." Also, in the movie The Social Network which chronicles his life, Mark is portrayed in his younger days as being socially awkward to the extent of exhibiting signs of autism. Not too long ago as well, a video of Zuckerberg breaking out in sweat and stammering while fielding questions on the D8 interview went viral on the internet. As a shy person who is socially awkward, Zuckerberg's most significant weakness in his early years as CEO of Facebook was communication, and that weakness could have inhibited his growth.

Today, however, Mark has mastered public speaking and has delivered moving addresses in Ivy League schools and even in parliament.

Strengths are those things in your nature that come naturally to you and which you can leverage to achieve success in your personal life and business. These strengths can manifest as inherent talents, acquired knowledge, character traits and skills.

Your weaknesses, on the other hand, are essential traits that do not come to you naturally. A great mentor will highlight those weaknesses to address. They are areas where you have inadequate knowledge and skills, poor, learned behavior and limited beliefs. Instead of being passive, you can learn to manage them or ultimately turn them to areas of strength. However, to turn your weaknesses to strengths and hone your powers to perfection, you need to be aware of them first.

As human beings that we are, we often compare ourselves with others around us and from this comparison, we feel superior or inferior to others based on our strengths and weaknesses and theirs. But the truth remains that all individuals are different. We have diverse temperaments and function differently based on our personalities. Some people can make angry customers happy in a jiffy while some others find joy in working alone. Some excel at drawing grand plans but are bad at executing same. I know entrepreneurs who are expert managers, but awful salespeople and I know others who find it tedious to sit in the office facing a screen; they would rather be out there pitching business and sealing sales deals.

Moreover, every personality type has its own merits and demerits. It is often said that "in our greatest strength lies our weaknesses, and in our weaknesses, there are strengths". How true is that? If you happen to be a decisive person who likes to take control and can easily give direction to others, you might tend to be bossy and to micromanage people. On the flip side, if you are the type who is quite understanding, and graciously empathetic, other people may see that as a leeway to take undue advantage of you.

Knowing your strengths and being aware of your weaknesses as an entrepreneur gives you a clear picture of how you would build your team. It gives you an inkling of the kind of people you need in your firm to complement your areas of weakness. For instance, if you are the type whose strength is operations and management, who will go out there to market and make the sales? And if you are the type who loves to swagger around town, always in search of the next deal, who manages the business when you are out there?

Gaining clarity on your strengths will put you in a better position to; focus on areas of your life where you can make the most significant impacts, boost your confidence and self-esteem, make better judgements and decisions and deliver more value to people around you. Similarly, as you become increasingly aware of your weaknesses, you will be able to manage them better thereby reducing the feelings of frustration and anxiety that comes with being unaware of those weaknesses. Also, you will be able to delegate tasks in your areas of weakness to individuals who are better positioned to handle them and then be able to focus more on things that will yield the highest returns.

Beyond knowing your weaknesses so that you can hire people to complement them in business, let it be clear that as a leader, there are some core abilities that you must master if by any chance they happen to be part of your weaknesses. Practical communication skills, emotional intelligence and the ability to make decisions are traits that you must not lack as a leader and which you cannot hire people to complement. Unlike marketing or project supervision that you can delegate, these three cannot be, and if you lack any of the three as a leader, you would be less efficient in the discharge of your duties, have great difficulty managing your team and relating with other stakeholders. It is only by maximizing your strengths and managing your weaknesses that you can build something of value which will give you the amount of wealth you desire, the level of freedom that you crave and the opportunity to change the world in the way you have always wanted to.

Now, I'll talk you through methods you can adopt to recognize your strengths and weaknesses.

Constructive Criticism

If there is one thing I have talked about extensively in this book, it is the importance of having a mentor. It can be quite daunting and excessively challenging to achieve success as an entrepreneur if you choose to go it all by yourself without the support a mentor. And thankfully, one of the benefits of having a mentor is that they can objectively and accurately point out your areas of strength and weakness to you, without fear or favor, after relating with you for a while. Beyond that, it is possible they might have encountered the same firm and weak traits in themselves or others close to them thereby putting them in a better position to give you advice on how to play to your strengths and work around the weaknesses.

Ask Your Employees

In today's data-driven world, humans (especially entrepreneurs) have become obsessed about measuring and analyzing just about anything; project outcomes, marketing campaigns, etc. And besides intangible things like the ones mentioned earlier, human performance can be measured and examined as well through what we refer to as "performance appraisals". Most bosses give appraisals without asking that they are appraised. As you evaluate the performance of your employees, provide them with the opportunity to appraise you as a leader so you can know your strengths and weaknesses to make necessary adjustments on how to be a better leader. You necessarily do not need to wait for periodic reviews. You can ask them what they think about your leadership style whenever you feel the need.

Though, for you to get the best out of any feedback mechanism from your employees, you have first to promote an environment that encourages them to be honest with you. If employees feel by telling you the hard truth, they may face retaliation, trust me, they will only exaggerate your strengths and lie about your weaknesses. In another vein, you can give them the chance to make their feedback anonymous if you so wish.

Learn from other Leaders

History can as well teach you a lot about how to discover your strengths and weaknesses. You can connect with past and present leaders by studying biographies, autobiographies, political texts, history books, etc. to learn about the different sides of leadership and how great leaders have lost and won their battles of strength and weakness. Moreover, you can connect with other business owners like you who can help you, as much as you support them, to know yourself better.

Self-Assessment

Today, there are so many free and paid online personality/psychology tests that you can take to discover your strengths and weaknesses. Fire up your laptop, log on to the world wide web and look for websites that offer such services.

Another angle to self-assessment is to keep a journal where you can document your thoughts and actions. After you have done this consistently for a while, go over all you have written again, and I bet you will discover specific patterns that will help you note your strengths and weaknesses.

Try Something New

Sometimes, many of the things we perceive to be weaknesses are merely things we have never tried or done before, and we can never indeed be able to classify such as strengths or weaknesses until we try them. Push yourself to do things that you have never done, and you will be surprised to see that specific thing you perceive as weaknesses are areas of strengths.

So, make it a core action point, before you go too thick in your entrepreneurial journey to identify your core strengths and the areas where you are weak. Having this important information up front and making necessary adjustments will significantly increase your productivity level and empower you to steer the affairs of your company in the direction of success and prosperity.

IDENTIFYING THE STRENGTHS AND WEAKNESSES OF YOUR EMPLOYEES

Discovering one's strengths and weaknesses are undoubtedly tricky, not to talk about helping others recognize theirs. The seeming difficult task is, however, worth the trouble as the knowledge and insight you gain about each team member can be pivotal to driving productivity and engagement in the workplace.

Great teams don't grow from the ground like groundnut or on trees like oranges; they take great efforts and substantial time to build. You as the boss, are the pacesetter in the organization and the task of making your team formidable rests on your shoulders, and there is no way you would be able to foster positive team relation and ensure optimum team performance if you are blind to the strengths and weaknesses of every employee. Furthermore, knowing the core strengths and limitations of each employee will help you make smarter decisions when it comes to assigning tasks and will ensure that each employee succeeds and find fulfilment in what they do thereby translate to greater success for the firm as well. Now, how can you accurately identify the strengths and weaknesses of your employees since merely asking, "what are your strengths and weaknesses?" during interviews or performance reviews may not do the trick - at both points, individuals are not likely, to be honest?

To start with, let it be known that for employees to be real and honest with you, you need to show them your human side first and also extend a hand of friendship. By candidly expressing your strengths and weaknesses first and asking their feedback about your style of leadership, you will earn their trust and they, in turn, will trust and open up to you about their strengths and vulnerabilities.

Above and below, listen to employees more, paying attention to how they generally behave (who is always jovial and who is still standoffish and quiet) and jotting down what you observe about each of your employees will help you establish patterns that reveal to you their real strengths and weaknesses.

Also, you can make your observation more objective by getting feedback from employees about the employee under scrutiny. Ask subjectively A what she thinks about B and vice versa. Match your evaluation against the information you gather from other employees to form objective and accurate judgements about the individual you are evaluating.

Since the goal of knowing the strengths and weaknesses of every employee is to help them become better, have a one-on-one conversation with each member of your team; discuss what you have observed to be their strong and weak points then work together with them to make necessary adjustments for their benefit and overall benefit of the company.

CHAPTER TEN

FINAL THOUGHTS

Since I have focused majorly on those who have become business owners already in most of the book, I deem it exigent to dedicate this part of the book to those who are still employees but seek ways to make extra cash on the side. Those who are new to the business of entrepreneurship and even need to earn extra money till the company starts paying the big bucks can also learn one or two tricks.

INTERNET BUSINESS IDEAS

Thanks to the internet, you can now make more than what your job pays you from gigs that require very little to no prior financial investment. A list of legitimate internet businesses you can engage in are as follows:

Forex Trading

Foreign exchange trading, popularly known as forex is a global market where investors trade currencies for trans-national investments. Today, we live in a globalized market where we need to exchange currencies to facilitate international trade. For instance, if you live in China and want to import a car from the United States, you need to convert your

Chinese Yuan to the dollar equivalent of the amount, because United States car dealerships will not accept Yuan. In the same vein, if an American goes to Santos on holiday, they will have to exchange their US dollars for the local Brazilian Reals.

Unlike in the past when the foreign exchange market was centralized to banks (especially central banks), the advent of the internet has however totally decentralized the market. Today, currencies are traded electronically over-the-counter (OTC) across all major financial centers in the world; New York, Singapore, Paris, Tokyo, Frankfurt and so on. The internet has made it possible for anyone to trade foreign exchange online on any of the numerous trading platforms available, 24 hours a day for five and a half days a week. With the internet connection, you can trade currencies that you own into other currencies with a view of selling them for a profit as prices change. And for your information, the forex market stays ahead of the stock market as the largest most liquid financial market in the whole world with about $4.9 trillion being traded on a daily basis, according to the Bank for International Settlements (BIS).

So, what are you waiting for? Go online, choose your most preferred platform and start to trade. Even if you know nothing about trading currencies before, there are websites that you can learn from. Some of these websites simulate real trading situations to ensure that you thoroughly understand the process.

Cryptocurrency Trading

Cryptocurrency trading works the same way as forex trading, but instead of trading fiat currencies like dollars, yen, naira and pound sterling, traders buy and sell cryptocurrencies like bitcoin, Litecoin and ether. Cryptocurrency traders can exchange cryptocurrencies to fiat currencies (US dollars to bitcoin) or transfer one cryptocurrency to another (ether to bitcoin) with the hope of making a profit.

Moreover, while commodities like gold can be traded only on weekdays and forex can be exchanged only five and a half days a week, cryptocurrencies are traded 24 hours a day, seven days a week. Also, there are various platforms online on which you can trade cryptocurrencies. Search online for a good one, create your account, buy some cryptocurrency with your credit card and start selling. You can, however, choose to be either a short term or long-term trader. Short term traders quickly take advantage of short-term price volatility to make a profit in hours or days while long-term traders hold currencies for periods spanning months and even years, studying the market for more extended periods to make informed trading decisions to avoid the loss that short-term trading can sometimes herald.

E-commerce

E-commerce means electronic commerce, i.e., the buying and selling of goods through the internet. With e-commerce, becoming a business merchant has never been easier. A few decades back, the import and export business would have required a significant investment of time and money, including but not limited to the hassle of traveling to foreign countries coupled with the language barriers to research and development. Without requiring a physical location, it's possible to earn a decent income that can be scaled without even having to supply inventory or deal with the challenges of warehousing and delivery. The overhead has been cut more than half by something called Dropshipping.

Dropshipping is one of the most common methods of e-commerce next to private labeling goods and/or selling goods based on arbitrage on eBay and Amazon. These platforms have digital payment platforms such as PayPal and Apple Pay, that allow you to transfer and receive money electronically and securely.

Drop shipping

Drop shipping is closely related to e-commerce in that it also does not require a physical location. The beauty of drop shipping, however, lies in the fact that you do not need to stock merchandise or own inventory to be in business. When you receive orders, all you need do is purchase the goods from a third party – usually a wholesale merchant or manufacturer – and have it delivered to the customer in your name. With this model, you most likely would not even see or handle products. It can easily be started by creating a Shopify account, a website and by setting up a Dropshipping vendor through Oberlo; an app that uses third party vendors such as a manufacturer from AliExpress as the drop shipper from China.

This industry has also evolved in the past few years as consumers' sentiments have been numbed by Dropshipping campaigns. Special marketing tactic and certain ad spend has to be implemented in order to see success in this business.

Print-on-demand

Print-on-demand essentially uses the drop shipping model. The difference between both is that while mainstream drop shipping allows you sell any merchandise without owning stock or inventory, print-on-demand makes it possible for you to sell products with your custom designs; t-shirts, umbrella, shoes, bags, mugs, etc. For example, let's say a client sees a t-shirt with your design online, loves it and sends you an order to supply 2,000 pieces, what you do is speak to a manufacturer, give them the model and they would print those 2,000 t-shirts with your custom design on it and have it shipped to the customer in your name. This also works with book publishing, especially for those who do not have the resources to fulfil large orders. If someone sees a book that you wrote and wants hundreds of copies, all you need do is speak to a book printer who will print the required number and send across to the customer on your behalf.

***

On a final note, the strategies for starting and scaling a successful business cannot be reduced to the pages of a book. Nonetheless, by reading this book, you have acquired some vital knowledge that imbues you with the mental habits and creative powers to help you seamlessly transition from employee to employer. With the information at your disposal, all that is left is for you to brace up and get into the ring. The amount of knowledge you acquire is useless without experience and practice. Remember that "the secret of getting ahead is getting started", in the words of Mark Twain. Successful entrepreneurs are self-motivated. They are doers and not dreamers and each moment you spend building another person's dream deducts from the time you have to create yours. There will never be a perfect time to start, and it is natural to be a bit hesitant and anxious. My final advice to you is to keep company close that encourages you to stay motivated and dedicated.

ABOUT THE AUTHOR

Henry Cheng is an entrepreneur, investor, consultant, co-founder of a private labeled wine and beer company, as well as a founder of a commercial insurance brokerage with head offices based in New York City. Having personal experience in start-ups and with his acquisitions of various ventures including insurance agencies, Henry has amassed a wealth of knowledge in assessing risk factors that apply from small to mid-tier business exposures. He serves as a consultant and advisor for his commercial clientele as a supplement to insuring their business risks. As an advocate of entrepreneurship, he understands first-hand the adversities young entrepreneurs have to deal with when trying to break free from mental and physical externalities.

www.henrychengofficial.com

Instagram: @hnkypnky

Twitter: @hnky_pnky

Facebook: @Hank P Cheng